D1298640

Inflation Hacking

Table of Contents

Disclaimer

While the author has taken the utmost effort to ensure the accuracy of the written content, all readers are advised to follow the information mentioned herein at their own risk. The author cannot be held responsible for any personal or commercial damage caused by the information. All readers are encouraged to seek professional advice when needed.

Investing is a risk, and you can lose money during times of high market volatility or bad individual company performance. No investment is guaranteed to make you money. And the best investments are generally personalized based on your individual cash flow and net worth. Ensure you consult a qualified financial advisor to ensure that you are adequately diversified and pick the investments that work for you.

Your Free Gift

We do want you to be best prepared for any inflationary shocks that might happen during this period. If you're trying to figure how to allocate your money, we have a $10000 free inflation portfolio below.

https://inflationportfolio.gr8.com/

Introduction to Inflation

Inflation is the rate at which a currency experiences a decrease in its purchasing power. It happens over a long period in most economies. However, there are examples of very high inflation rates over short periods, known as hyperinflation. Economists argue that inflation is almost always a result of an excessive increase in the money supply in an economy.

The general population feels inflation by the increase in the prices of goods they purchase. Things like groceries, fuel, and utilities get expensive over the length of time when an economy is experiencing inflation. Each unit of that economy's currency loses its value in terms of what people can exchange it for. When economies continue to suffer relatively high inflation rates over long periods, people can afford fewer things. If they have money saved in interest-free bank accounts, the value of their savings also decreases.

What causes inflation?

When there is more money available, and the quantity of goods remains the same, the demand for money will be lower and basic economics will apply. Now, people would be willing to pay more money for the same item, which will cause an increase in the price of that item. An increase in the overall money supply would mean that buyers can pay more for the same things across the board. As a result, there is an increase in the price of items, and the economy will experience inflation. They refer to an imbalance between the money required by an economy for its trade-related needs and the amount of money supplied. It is worth mentioning that an overall sustained increase in prices has to occur for inflation. A singular rise in prices due to demand does not point towards inflation. Even though most economists agree that an increased money supply is the main reason behind inflation, there are three key drivers of inflation when the supply of money increases.

Demand-Pull Effect

This phenomenon occurs when the population suddenly has a lot more money to spend. Naturally, the demand for items increases. When this demand is unmet by the manufacturers and producers of goods, the demand for goods increases, causing the demand to drive up prices.

Cost-Push Effect

This effect occurs when the demand-pull effect applies to intermediary goods such as oil, utilities, and other raw materials. As the retailers factor in these costs when they price their products, an increase in their price causes an increase in the finished goods' price.

Built-In Inflation

This effect is a result of an economy that has been experiencing inflation for a long time. Employers increase their wages to accommodate the trends. When their wages increase, the cost of labor increases for the producers and manufacturers. This causes an increase in the price of finished goods.

How do economists determine the rate of inflation?

Economists can model inflation trends and can make projections for future economic periods. They do this by various methods. One is by looking at historical data and using macroeconomic changes to produce a forecast for the future. These forecasts help Governments and Central Banks monitor their monetary and fiscal policies, respectively.

The metric used to measure inflation is the Consumer Price Index (CPI). To calculate the CPI, determine the weighted average of a basket of everyday consumer goods and services such as food, healthcare, transportation, etc. It calculates how the average price of these products and services change over time. This gives a general idea of the rate of inflation an economy is experiencing.

As we have explained earlier, inflation is an increase in the prices of a basket of everyday items that change over time. That makes it a lot easier for almost everyone to determine the rate of inflation in their region. However, it's important to remember that the inflation rate you calculate may not be the same as the one determined by your regional or national government. The main reason for this is that those institutions will most definitely be using a basket of goods that will be quite different from yours. For example, they might be taking the average price of unbranded wheat or rice, whereas you would be comparing a specific rice brand that you use regularly. Let us look at different large economies that measure their respective CPIs.

United States

In the US, the Bureau of Labor Statistics determines the CPI. The Bureau collects samples of tens of thousands of products that get purchased by thousands of families across the United States to track their prices. They look at all types of products and services for this exercise. They do this by selecting a popular item through a process called initiation. For example, they can choose a specific brand for a particular type of cheese purchased by a large number of families in the US. The sample product changes every four years. The statistics are in the link below:

https://www.bls.gov/cpi/

Australia

The Australian Bureau of Statistics is responsible for the calculation of the Australian CPI. It determines the CPI by calculating the change in thousands of everyday items' prices and grouping them into 87 categories and 11 broad groups. The bureau then tracks the difference in these items' prices every quarter and then publishes the CPI. The 11 groups are housing, food/non-alcoholic beverages, Transport, Recreation and culture, Alcohol and tobacco, Furnishings, household equipment and services, Health, Education, Insurance and financial services,

Communication, Clothing, and footwear. The statistics are in the link below:

https://www.abs.gov.au/statistics/economy/price-indexes-and-inflation/consumer-price-index-australia

Here are the links to inflation data for other major world economies.

China

https://data.worldbank.org/indicator/FP.CPI.TOTL.ZG?locations=CN

Japan

https://www.stat.go.jp/english/data/cpi/

Germany

https://www.destatis.de/EN/Themes/Economy/Prices/Consumer-Price-Index/_node.html

United Kingdom

https://www.ons.gov.uk/economy/inflationandpriceindices

India

http://mospi.nic.in/cpi

France

https://data.worldbank.org/indicator/FP.CPI.TOTL.ZG?locations=FR

Brazil

https://data.worldbank.org/indicator/FP.CPI.TOTL.ZG?locations=BR

Canada

https://www.statcan.gc.ca/eng/subjects-start/prices_and_price_indexes/consumer_price_indexes

How You Can Measure Inflation Yourself

Measurement of inflation is very complex, and there are many ways to measure it. Different metrics can give you different results. Since every person spends money on different items, inflation is different for every person or family.
Let us discuss how you can determine the rate of inflation to an accurate degree on your own to become more aware of how much you are spending and if you need to take any steps towards protecting your financing against the harmful effects of inflation.

The best way to calculate inflation at home is to track the prices of the goods and services you use regularly. As a result, you will determine how inflation directly impacts you instead of how general inflation affects other people. You can calculate inflation by following the steps given below.

- Create a selection of everyday goods and services you use. For example:
  - 1kg of your favorite brand's rice or flour.
  - Price of a fixed unit of your favorite snack, e-g, a chocolate bar.
  - Your monthly mobile phone cost.

- Your monthly price of utilities.
- Price of a movie ticket at your local cinema.
- Price of 1 liter (or gallon) of fuel in your area.
- Price of a private medical check-up in your area.

These prices should be easy to collect every month. You can track the changes in these prices on a quarterly, semi-annually, or yearly basis to see how much they have increased. You can then see the rate at which prices rise with inflation in your area. An example calculation could be as follows.

Price of 1kg rice on January 1st, 2021: $4
Price of 1kg rise on March 1st, 2021: $4
Price of 1kg rise on June 1st, 2021: $4.2
Price of 1kg rice on September 1st, 2021: $4.2
Price of 1kg rice on January 1st, 2022: $4.5

Inflation calculated on a semiannual basis:

January-June 2021: (4.2-4)/4% = 5%

The inflation rate was 5% on a semi-annual basis between January and June of 2021, taking rice as an example.

Do the same for all items in your list and calculate the average rate of inflation.

Why do some economists think inflation is good?

Businesses rely on a steady stream of cash flow to function. They count on constant sales to become and stay profitable. Ongoing sales are only possible if people keep spending money. People make purchases mostly because of specific needs, but they also make purchases to benefit from lower prices. Just look at how incredibly successful sales are for business.

What exactly does a sale imply? It implies that if you don't purchase an item during a given time frame, its price will increase. Inflation essentially acts as a massive sale for most, if not all, items in an economy. People believe that spending now is better than spending in the future because prices will increase. Also, prices increase while wages do not. This results in people spending more instead of saving, which keeps the businesses going.

An economy with many thriving businesses continues to grow, creating more employment opportunities, increasing wages, and raising living standards for people. Those economists who believe that a low rate of inflation is beneficial to an economy support this view.

How Inflation Can Hurt You

We have explained earlier that inflation causes a rise in the price of items. These items are all sorts of things you use daily, such as food, utilities, clothes, and fuel. However, inflation also causes increases in prices of essential and emergency services such as healthcare, transportation, education, and insurance. The important thing is that all modern economies experience inflation. However, your financial circumstances might not survive high rates of inflation.

You could lose your job, or your business might suffer a loss, consequently reducing your income. However, even if you have a stable job, your purchasing power will decrease if your wages do not increase over time. You will be unable to afford the same quantity of items that you could only a few years back, your rent will increase, which eats into your expendable income, and any savings you have in the bank will lose their value over time.

How to safeguard your finances against inflation?

We have discussed in detail what inflation is. It is essentially the value of your money going down over time. Another way to look at it is that the value of items goes up over time. The logical way to protect your finances against inflation is to invest in items instead of cash. But that is easier said than done. With hundreds of asset classes to choose from, it might become so confusing that you might end up with your standard savings account. But investing in assets, bonds or commodities should not be this hard. We certainly do not think so. The next sections of this book will discuss different types of assets that protect against inflation. We will discuss how you can invest in these and the characteristics of those assets that enable them to act as a suitable hedge against inflation.

Precious Metals

Precious metals are those metals that have a remarkably high value compared to other metals. This higher price can result from various factors such as scarcity, use in industrial applications, and market sentiment. Investors have long used precious metals to hedge against not only inflation but also adverse market risks. The price of precious metals usually rises in times of economic certainty because investors choose to buy them as 'safe-havens.' This means that they are considered safer than other asset classes, such as equities. However, the prices of precious metals increase over the long term anyway.

Precious metals are almost always easy to purchase. They are easy to store because of how little space they take when physically stored. They also have reasonably high liquidity, which means that they can be sold for cash whenever required. These factors make precious metals an excellent choice for an asset class to hedge against inflation. We will discuss a few precious metals in detail below.

Gold

Gold is by far the most famous metal to ever exist. Humans have been in love with Gold for as long as we can trace record history. It was always thought to be valuable and has maintained its status as an undisputed safe-haven asset for many millennia and continues to maintain its position even today. Investors use Gold to diversify risk in their portfolios, hedge against inflation, and safeguard against worst-case scenarios such as war. It has long been considered a store of value, and continued to rise in value throughout history.

Why does Gold have value?

Gold has held steady value throughout time, which is why it is often relied on as a hedge during tough times. It has importance as part of a diversified investment portfolio. Gold's value can increase in response to events that cause a decline in the value of paper investments (stocks and bonds) to decline. Although short-term volatility in Gold's price is almost inevitable, it has always maintained its value over the long term, thus offering an excellent investment opportunity.

How effective is Gold against inflation?

As we quote Gold against the U. S. dollar, the dollar value loss due to inflation makes Gold more expensive. This expensive Gold provides a hedge against inflation. Moderate inflation levels do not affect gold prices, which tend to remain stable, but high inflation rates lead to higher gold prices. This makes it an effective hedge during inflationary periods, especially in the long run.

Below you can see the performance of Gold over the last 100 years. You see the outstanding performance of Gold during the 1970s. The 1970s were not only a highly inflationary period, but it was also the period where the US Government removed the US dollar link to Gold.

Over the last 100 years, the growth rate has been 4.5% per year, which is higher than the average annual rate of inflation in the United States (3%).

2021 = $1850

1921 = $20.61

Rate of growth = 4.5% per year

How can you invest in Gold?

You can purchase Gold in several ways. You can buy physical gold bullion from traders and online stores. You can also invest in Exchange Traded Funds that have a significant quantity of Gold in their portfolios. You can also purchase Gold on the commodities market online.

Silver

Silver is a rare metal with a lot of versatility. It was one of the first native metals to be mined. Crafting jewelry and making currency, silverware, dental fillings, and mirrors are just a few ways we use Silver. Silver iodide seeds clouds that can produce rainfall. In addition to its antibacterial properties, it also offers several health benefits. Silver is the best conductor, so it has significant industrial use. Other applications include the manufacture of contacts, switches, and fuses. The value of silver is of little wonder.

Why does Silver have value?

Silver has long been a form of money and a store of value. Today, it has become the most widely used coin-making material ever. The continuing cognizance of silver and its store of value have maintained the worth of silver over the centuries. As it has moved out of currency, silver supply and demand are primarily rooted in jewelry, industrial applications, and investment options.

How effective is Silver against inflation?

Silver remains an affordable asset for investors as a hedge against inflation. With a lower price point than Gold, it can be more appealing to the smaller retail investor. With its correlation to stocks and bonds, it can be an excellent asset to diversify a portfolio. Due to its industrial applications, the price of silver moves more with inflation, requiring a much smaller investment to hedge against inflation.

Below is the 100-year chart for Silver. It shows a growth of **3.7% per year**, which slightly outpaces the inflation rate. Silver is undervalued when compared to Gold.

Source: Macrotrends

2021 Price = $25

1921 Price = $0.61

Rate of growth = 3.7% per year

How can you invest in Silver?

There are multiple ways to invest in Silver. The traditional method involves buying actual bullion bars bought and sold over the counter at major banks. Additionally, investments can be made in silver coins and rounds, silver exchange-traded products, a silver certificate of ownership in place of actual bullions, silver accounts allowing direct buying and selling of silver, and in the form of investment in silver mining companies.

Platinum

Platinum is a scarce precious metal known for its strong conductivity, resistance to corrosion, and durability. It has tremendous economic importance, and its applications include jewelry, catalytic converters, oil refining, electronics, and dentistry. A diverse range of applications has ensured high demand for Platinum, with a resulting significant economic role.

Why does Platinum have value?

Although Platinum has a short financial history, having been discovered only about 300 years ago, its scarcity often confers its value. The rarity of platinum deposits and the difficulty in mining them has made it the highest symbol of value and quality. It has become a significant attraction for investors looking to diversify their portfolios. Platinum is mostly in one country, South Africa, which limits its availability. Moreover, the imbalance in the limited supply and excess demand of Platinum lends it even greater value.

How effective is Platinum against inflation?

It has been identified as a moderately good investment for portfolio diversification and hedging against inflation. It is traded around the clock on global markets and often tends to fetch a much higher price than Gold in financially and politically stable periods. Due to its intrinsic value and correlation to stocks and bonds, even a small percentage of Platinum can offer inflationary protection.

Below is the 50-year-old chart for Platinum. As you can see, it does increase over time. The rate of increase tends to match the rate of inflation. However, an important thing to note in the chart is the peaks. The peaks happen at different times as compared to Gold and Silver. So, a small position in Platinum can hedge against inflation and serve as a great diversifier in your precious metals portfolio.

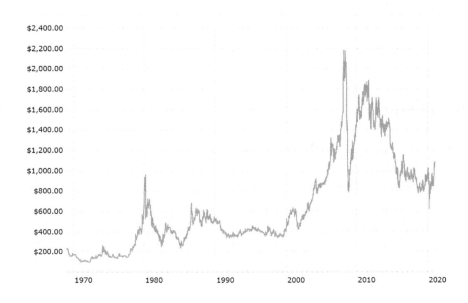

Source: Macrotrends

2020 Price = $1029

1970 Price = $226

Rate = **3.1% per year**

How can you invest in Platinum?

Platinum is traded as an exchange-traded fund (ETF) on the London and New York stock exchanges, offering a good investment vehicle. Platinum is also available in the form of coins and bars available at different foundries, as well as in the form of Platinum accounts where it can be instantly bought or sold. Another way is to create a futures contract where Platinum is bought or sold at a predetermined time and place.

Palladium

Palladium might not be the most popular precious metal, but it is a highly effective asset for investment to protect against inflation. It is the fourth precious metal we will discuss in this. As a by-product of Platinum mining, Palladium holds immense investment value.

Why does Palladium have value?

The industrial, jewelry and investment usages of Palladium have contributed to its sporadic growth and value. It has quickly become the most valuable of the four precious metals, primarily due to its application in the automotive industry as a raw material in hybrid vehicles' catalytic converters. Acute shortages have also driven Palladium prices up. With climate change and antipollution policies in effect worldwide, demand for Palladium has only increased, and it has been trading above Gold for the past year. Its value is also derived mainly from its application as an inflation hedge.

How effective is Palladium against inflation?

Like other precious metals, Palladium is also priced in U. S. dollars, giving it an inverse relation to the dollar. Therefore, appreciation in the dollar rarely influences Palladium, and depreciation in the dollar reduces purchasing power, making metals like Palladium an ideal hedge against inflation. Palladium has been steadily increasing in value since the start of the 21st century, which has greatly benefited investors.

In the Palladium chart below, you can see that it is the best performing of the precious metals with a growth rate of 8.7%; due to the increasing demand for palladium. Palladium has applications in catalytic converters of automobiles, and consumers are shifting away from diesel to petrol vehicles recently, which is great for palladium in the short term. But remember that if electric vehicles increase their market share, it might hurt palladium in the long term. So, it's best not to have a considerable investment in Palladium.

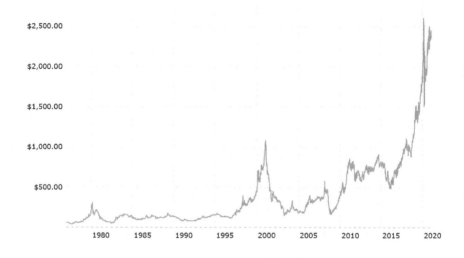

Source: Macrotrends

2020 price = $2365

1970 price = $58.5

Rate = **8.8% per year**

How can you invest in Palladium?

Investors may gain exposure to palladium by investing in palladium-focused businesses. Direct investment in Palladium producers includes Norilsk Nickel, North American Palladium, Stillwater Mining. Alternatively, investors can buy bullion bars and coins made of Palladium for portfolio growth. Exchange-traded funds are also a good investment vehicle. Palladium-backed ETFs track the precious metal like an index fund but trading on a stock exchange.

Gold Mining Companies

Since gold prices are the same everywhere, companies with lower costs per ounce of gold mined to make the most profit. The gold mining stock price is mostly contingent on Gold's price, especially with companies whose primary business is gold mining. That said, gold mining companies can produce lucrative output for investors.

Why do Gold Mining Companies have value?

The value of gold mining companies is derived mainly from the value of the Gold. Their primary worth comes in their ability to offer the potential of leveraged upside to Gold's price. When gold prices rise, mining companies can increase their total production to grow their total sales. There is also a strong relationship between the price of Gold and gold mining stock. A 10% increase in gold bullion price can translate into a 20-30% increase in stock prices. Limited supply also poses barriers to entry, which further lends to the value of mining companies

How effective are Gold Mining Companies against inflation?

Gold mining stocks provide a hedge against inflation. Gold rises with inflation but typically also produces earnings in non-inflationary times. Therefore, gold mining stocks offer a better inflationary hedge than base metal mining stocks, as higher prices translate into higher profits. However, over-taxation of companies in inflationary times can sometimes reduce earnings. Gold mining stocks also provide a broader portfolio and gold investments, reducing overall volatility and increasing risk tolerance.

How can you invest in Gold Mining Companies?

Gold mining companies are available as shares on the stock market. The decision to invest in a particular gold mining company should be an informed one supported by understanding the mining industry's cyclical nature. Additionally, investors should identify companies who can weather inevitable downturns with low production costs and strong balance sheets.

Gold Streaming Companies

Gold streaming companies act as middlemen in the gold mining sector. They pay an upfront fee to mining companies in exchange for a percentage of their revenue or a right to purchase their future production at a fixed cost. Their investment aids cash-strapped mining companies in exploration and production projects, which grants gold streaming companies exposure to a range of companies in the gold sector.

Why do Gold Streaming Companies have value?

Despite a rise in metal prices, investors still prefer to buy stocks from streaming companies than gold mining companies. The extensive exposure range makes streaming companies a much safer, more reliant investment, and they hold their value in the lower-risk investment they offer. As bigger gold miners are fully valued, this practically makes streaming companies the more attractive investment choice.

How effective are Gold Streaming Companies against inflation?

The lower risk involved in gold streaming companies makes them a good hedge against inflation. The interest rate and production upside can typically provide a return on investment, even if Gold itself is shorted as a hedge. Streaming companies have been trading at all-time highs even when mining companies were trading at all-time lows. Gold streaming companies have even reported increased dividends. Despite the poor price performance of mining companies, streaming company performance has remained unharmed. As streaming companies hold highly diversified portfolios of mines and other assets, the concentration mitigates risk.

How can you invest in Gold Streaming Companies?

Stocks for various gold streaming companies are available on the stock exchange. Some of the largest streaming companies include *Wheaton Precious Metals, Franco-Nevada, Royal Gold, Osisko Mining,* and *Sandstorm Gold.* Investment decisions should be the product of thorough research into the company's performance and risk mitigation abilities, although diversification primarily assures low risk.

Gold Mining vs. Gold Streaming Performance

Below is a chart of the Gold Miners VanEck ETF vs. SPDR Gold Shares ETF since 2000. As you can see, Gold Miners do underperform the value of Gold ETFs because most Gold mining companies are poorly run and inefficient.

Investments in Gold Mining companies require a lot of expertise in individual gold mining companies and about the gold market in general. Finding the right investment at the right time is the key to success in gold mining companies, but investing in Gold or gold ETF seems like a safer bet.

- SPDR® Gold Shares Total Return Price % Change
- VanEck Vectors Gold Miners ETF Total Return Price % Change

Source: Lyn Alden Investment Strategy, www.lynaden.com

In the chart below, we compare the performance of 3 popular Gold Streaming companies vs. Gold Etf (Gold ETF is in purple). As you can see, all the Gold Streaming companies outperform Gold.

Gold Streaming companies, in general, are a significant investment and the best way to invest in Gold.

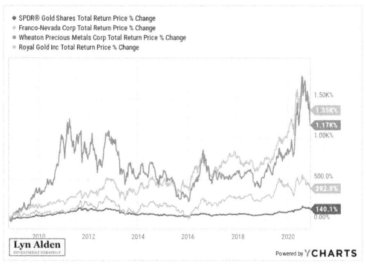

Source: Lyn Alden Investment Strategy, www.lynaden.com

Commodities

Commodities are those goods that investors perceive to have value without giving any significance to their origin or brand. For example, wheat can be grown in any part of the United States, and it would get traded as wheat. Most of these goods are in constant demand throughout the world, such as cocoa, oil, rice, cotton, and copper.

Commodities are an asset class that is traded almost exactly like securities. They are available on unique exchanges called mercantile exchanges. Investors typically group commodities into two main categories, soft commodities and hard commodities. They refer to soft commodities as cultivated goods, such as wheat, corn, and soybeans, or ranched goods, such as cattle. And they refer to hard commodities as goods that require drilling or mining to extract from the earth, such as oil.

Why do commodities perform well against inflation?

As we explained earlier, inflation reduces the purchasing power of a currency. Another way to look at it is that things become more expensive. Items that are in demand all the time become more expensive consistently, which is where commodities come in. When you invest in commodities, you are essentially trading in your currency that will devalue over time because of inflation and getting something that will increase in value. If you keep your investments in commodities over a long period, they will almost always provide an effective hedge against inflation.

Oil

Oil is arguably the most important source of energy we have today. Even after various power plants shifting towards renewable sources, oil dominates the transportation sector. It continues to be the primary source of plastic.

Why does oil have value?

Oil is the top energy source for the world today. Countries such as the United States and China consumed a combined 33 million barrels per day in 2019. These countries also like to keep large reserves of oil for future uses, and because for all other countries that are not exporters also need oil, oil has a consistent demand. This is true even when oil loses value because other factors (mostly speculative) determine oil's value.

How effective is oil against inflation?

Besides the abnormal price actions such as the one in 2014 and 2020, oil can still offer protection against inflation in the short term. Investing in oil directly might not be the best way to protect yourself against inflation as the oil markets can be very volatile. However, let's look at oil-focused ETF and especially the energy companies such as Exxon and BP. We can see a very healthy appreciation in value when checking their share price performance. Both Exxon and BP experienced incredible gains between 2010 and the start of 2020 by almost doubling the price. Exxon's share price was 56.57 on 2nd July 2010 and jumped to 102.65 just four years later.

The historical chart below shows that oil tends to track within $20 - $140 per barrel. So, it's best to invest in oil companies when it is close to the lower end and sell closer to the top end of the range.

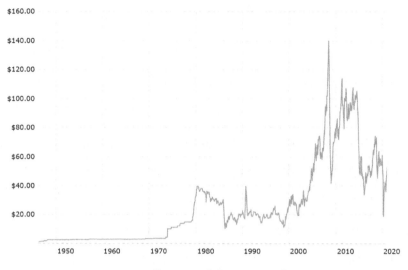

Source: Macrotrends

How can you invest in oil?

The safest way to invest in oil is by investing in oil-focused ETFs and large energy companies. These companies understand the risks associated with oil as an investment, and how to manage the risks. Keep in mind that oil might serve to be a short-term hedge against inflation because of the changing trend towards energy sources for the future.

Copper

Copper has remained an integral part of the industry for thousands of years. Once can mold copper into various shapes, due to its' highly malleable nature; making copper an excellent choice of metal for wires and motors. It is an excellent heat and electricity conductor, making it a viable option for various other industrial uses.

Why does copper have value?

Copper has applications in almost all types of industries throughout the world. Investors who trade copper speculate on the global demand due to an ever-increasing industrial activity. More recently, in growing economies like India and China, copper demand outpaced copper production. The growth of the housing market also contributes towards increasing demand for copper due to its electrical uses. Investors continue to value copper as a reliable hedge against inflation. It is also used heavily to manufacture motors, investors, batteries, and wiring for electric vehicles. The average use of copper by weight per vehicle is 83KG, and with electric vehicle demand expected to increase in the coming years, copper will remain a precious commodity.

How effective is copper against inflation?

According to Bloomberg intelligence, copper consistently outperformed every other primary asset class except energy when measured against every 1% annual increase in the United States

Consumer Price Index. Its base trading per pound increased by almost 50% between December 2016 and December 2018.

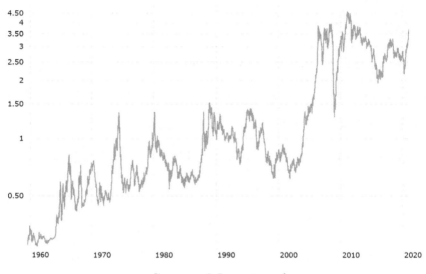

Source: Macrotrends

The historical chart of copper above shows an average increase of approximately 4% per year, which outpaces inflation. Copper offers a lot more future promise due to its use in electric vehicles and construction projects.

How can you invest in copper?

Copper is an excellent long-term hedge against inflation when traded individually. Its lot size may be an issue as it comes in a

25,000 pounds lot. So, if the trading price for one pound were 3 USD, you would need to invest 75,000 USD. However, the best way to invest in copper is by investing in copper mining companies. These companies make their livelihoods from copper and have better measures in place, which provide more stable returns than the metal itself.

Corn

Corn is among the most popular global food sources. A crop native to Central America, corn has been grown in almost all parts of the world for centuries. It is used as a food source, making ethanol, producing high fructose corn syrup, and producing a variety of alcoholic drinks. The United States is the largest corn producer, with an annual production of over 350 Million Metric Tons.

Why does corn have value?

Global demand for food continues to grow by the day, which is met with various food sources. One of these is corn. Corn continues to remain in high demand in the United States, China, and the European Union for various purposes. Ethanol demand is an important price driving factor for corn as various Governments have to meet biofuel targets. Its price is related to the price of oil, and if oil prices rise, ethanol will become an even more attractive fuel source which would drive up the price of corn. With increasing temperatures due to global warming, corn output gets easily affected. A lower corn supply results, and corn gets more expensive.

How effective is corn against inflation?

Corn is an excellent hedge against inflation because of its various price drivers and its overall global requirement as a food source. Because of the food source point, inflation will inevitably cause its price to rise. Owning corn instead of currency will provide the required protection against inflation. Corn has consistently proved to be less volatile than other grains such as wheat and soy, making it a more stable long-term investment.

Below is the long-term chart for corn prices. The long-term chart shows that though corn prices have increased, they haven't kept pace with inflation. The reason for this is that improvements in technology are a strong deflationary force for food prices.

It is best to be careful with investing in corn producers, being very selective in choosing companies with high cash flow, and investing during times when they are corn shortages due to an external stimulus. Investing in corn can be a good diversifier during certain times.

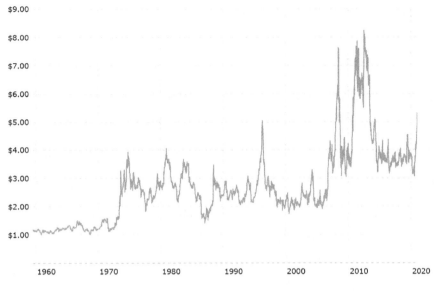

Source: Macrotrends

How can you invest in corn?

You can invest in corn in a variety of ways. The first and foremost option is futures contracts and options. Although these are speculative instruments, they can provide the necessary hedge against inflation if the price moves in your intended direction. A less-speculative mode of investment is to invest in corn-focused ETFs and companies. There are no companies that purely deal with corn. However, the companies you should be looking for are those that are in business with corn producers. Producers of fertilizers, pesticides, and animal feeds can be viable investment options.

Wheat

Wheat is cultivated worldwide for its cereal grain seed, a staple for almost every country. Wheat stems from a grass type referred to as Triticum grown in numerous places worldwide. Wheat happens to be the most widely cultivated food crop on land, used mainly for bread, different kinds of pasta, and other bakery goods. China, Pakistan, USA are some of the top wheat-producing and exporting countries in the world.

Why does wheat have value?

Wheat is the powerhouse of starch and energy, with components, like protein and vitamins essential for health. It is an important carbohydrate source for most countries. It is easily digested and can be highly nutritious when combined with other proteins. Wheat, alongside maize and rice, plays a significant contribution in supplying food to the nearly 9 billion in the world today. People cultivate wheat worldwide, and its worldwide demand is the primary reason behind its universal appeal.

How effective is wheat against inflation?

Regardless of a country's economic conditions, wheat continues to appeal to all and is an excellent investment. It gets ample attention because of constant global demand. Similar to other commodities, wheat poses an attractive investment opportunity while being an inflationary hedge. With rising prices, raw materials and food commodities such as wheat also rise. Wheat, being a necessity of a large number of the world's diet, allows it to remain attractive to investors in inflationary period.

While inflation can be dangerous for various other investments, the opposite is true with commodities. The increase in wheat value allows investors to balance their losses that they may have experienced elsewhere. Wheat is used widely for food production, making it a potent inflationary hedge.

From the historical chart, we see that food prices have increased with time; but have not kept pace with inflation.

Diversifying with small investments in strong wheat-producing companies can serve a purpose at certain times of high inflation. We can see considerable increases in wheat prices during the early 1970s and late 2000s due to increased money supply in the economy.

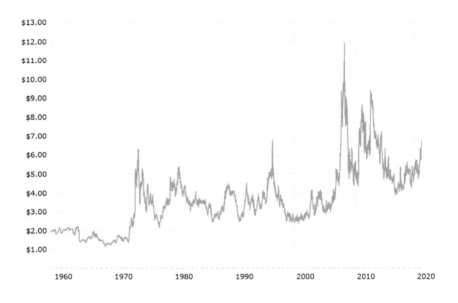

Source: Macrotrends

How can you invest in wheat?

To hedge against inflation, you can consider investing in wheat. The most straightforward way to invest in wheat is through wheat options like other commodities. Options allow you to speculate on wheat prices and enable you to pick a position according to your level of risk.

You can also invest in stocks of companies that deal directly with wheat, such as cereal producers, fertilizer manufacturers, and agricultural machinery manufacturers like John Deere.

Lumber

Lumber refers to wood that is available such as planks and beams, after being processed. It trades on mercantile exchanges like other commodities. Its main uses are in residential and commercial construction, for various flooring purposes, and manufacturing furniture. Major lumber producers are the United States, Russia, China, and Canada. All of these producers have large swathes of the forest for lumber production.

Why does lumber have value?

Lumber is by far the most used construction material in the United States, which, along with China, are the two largest lumber-consuming countries. Global demand for lumber also remains high and is expected to grow. This is primarily driven by the ever-increasing demand for residential and commercial properties, wood furnishings, and various kinds of wood-dependent furniture.

How effective is lumber against inflation?

Lumber prices soared in 2020. Between early March and October 2020, lumber's price increased from around 280 USD to over 900 USD, which is an excellent indication of how lumber performs when the market is experiencing extreme levels of uncertainty. The ever-growing pressure from environmentalists against the reduction of forest cover is a strong driver of lumber's price. Trees do not grow as fast as crops, so the race to make logging sustainable gets faster every year, which consistently drives lumber's price upwards. These reasons make lumber a relatively much better hedge against inflation than other commodities. Below is the historical chart for lumber. It usually has a steady price, but at certain times, we see substantial price hikes. For example, in 2020, there was a considerable increase in demand for lumber due to people doing more home renovation, which saw lumber hit all-time highs in 2020.

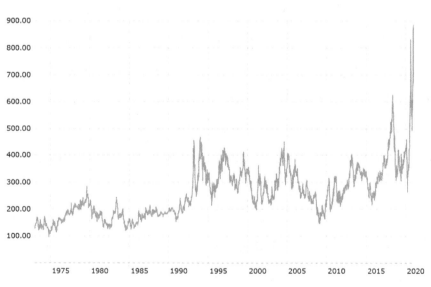

Source: Macrotrends

How can you invest in lumber?

Lumber trades in planks per 1000 board feet. Online investment portals allow you to trade lumber futures and options. As always, these are speculative instruments that can incur a loss if the price does not move in your favor. However, hedging against inflation is a long-term investment, and small price changes will not affect the overall long-term performance. Lumber stocks are an excellent investment if you do not want to invest in lumber directly. Various listed companies engaged in logging have provided consistent value appreciation over the years and can be viable options for hedging against inflation.

Cotton

Its universal application as a textile raw material has ensured a thriving global trade for cotton. According to the World Wildlife Fund (WWF), cotton is the most widespread, non-food profitable crop globally. Its role in the global textile and fashion industries, cosmetics industry, pharmaceuticals, in addition to its industrial applications, make it a worthy investment commodity to consider.

Why does cotton have value?

Demand and supply dynamics for cotton largely influence its trading price. Based on these factors, economists have projected a moderate, steady growth of the cotton sector. Given its demand, cotton has a large and relatively stable presence on the stock market, making it a preferred investment choice. Cotton investment also allows for exposure to other agricultural commodities and offers a great way to broaden a portfolio.

How effective is cotton against inflation?

As global economies grow, commodities like cotton grow with them. With a finite supply of cotton, limited by seasonal changes, cotton is more likely to retain its value and act as a hedge against inflation. Cotton has a statistically high hedging potential against inflation, with a positive correlation between inflation rates and asset returns. It performs exceptionally well in long-term investments.

The historical chart shows that cotton price hasn't increased because of better technologies to manufacture cotton. Cotton can be a good diversifier during periods of high inflation, but investments need to made in strong producers with high cash flow at specific periods.

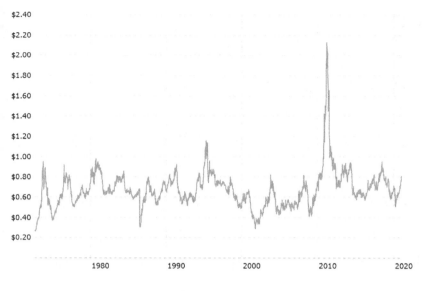

How can you invest in cotton?

A standard option for cotton investment is stocks. Stocks run a lower risk middle-ground between more direct options. They can be bought directly in cotton manufacturing companies or textile-based companies that use cotton as a raw material. On the other hand, Cotton ETFs offer the benefit of a bundle of assets; due to diversification, market movements have less influence on ETF performance. Additionally, you can invest in cotton futures through regular brokerage accounts, which can be very profitable.

Strategy

As you can see, most commodities increase over time; but don't always keep up with inflation. This is because of the increase in technology and the decay of commodities over time. Precious metals don't decay, but commodities do. Thus, it's best to avoid a buy and hold strategy for commodities.

My favorite strategy is a buy low, sell high strategy. Buy when the commodity is cheap (relative to the M2 money supply) and sell when high. Many producers also tend to have decent dividends, so factor in the dividend when analyzing the stock benefits.

Strong Currency

A strong currency can effectively protect you against inflation. The simple logic behind this is that inflation will cause your cash holdings to lose value. To retain the same value of your holdings or to experience an increase, you will need more of the currency you use to spend. To get more of your local currency without investing in any other asset classes, you can purchase a currency of another country that has historically performed better than your local currency. When your country experiences inflation, its exchange rate will also get affected as the local currency will lose its value. This means that other countries' currencies will gain value against your local currency. This implies that even if the other country's currency has not improved in value on its own, it will still be a better option as you can get of your local currency after it has devalued.

How to evaluate the strength of a currency?

The simplest way to assess the value of a currency is to compare it with another currency. Currencies are always traded in pairs, and their values are represented in this way as well. The USD, for example, has no value on its own unless it is used to purchase another currency or to purchase goods. To value the US Dollar, we would need to determine how much of another currency we can buy with 1 USD. If the currency we want to purchase is the British pound, then we would need to see how many US dollars we will get for one British pound. Whatever value we get for this will be the exchange rate of the British pound with the US dollar and will be traded as a pair called GBP/USD. If you were buying British pounds for US dollars on the 12th of December 2020, you would need 1.32 USD for every GBP.

To determine the strength of a currency, we would need to look at the history of the price of a currency pair over a period of time. This trend will tell us how a currency has fared against another over a specific period of time. A strong currency will experience an increase in its value against another currency over a period of time. Taking the example of the GBP/USD pair, if the 1.32 value decreased to 1.16 over a 6-month period, you would need fewer dollars to buy the same number of pounds. In this case, you will 1 dollar and 16 cents instead of 1 dollar and 32 cents to purchase one British pound. This means that the British pound would have gotten weaker against the US dollar.

The main driving forces behind currency value appreciation are the demand of the currency as well as the ability of a country to register a trade surplus year on year. A trade surplus means that it earns more foreign exchange than it uses. This results in the country having an excess of a foreign currency, in most cases the USD, which results in the value of its own currency getting higher. A prime example is the Norwegian Krone which has experienced an increase in value over the past five years against the USD.

Example of strong currencies in past periods

With over 175 currencies traded in the forex markets every day, there are plenty of options to choose from. However, when we are talking about protecting against inflation, we must consider how certain currencies have performed over the years against our local currency. Having said that, some currencies are considered safe havens regardless of where you live. This is because these currencies experience appreciation in their value due to a number of other factors that are global while also being consistent.

United States Dollar

The United States Dollar has historically been a great safe-haven currency for non-US investors and remains immensely popular amongst them. It is mostly ideal for investors whose home currencies have performed poorly against the USD historically. It is an excellent diversifier for those in non-US countries with weaker currencies. However, the USD has not performed as other stronger currencies in terms of its intrinsic value, such as the Kuwaiti Dinar or the Omani Riyal. The Federal Reserve Bank of New York is an institution of the United States Government and the only body that can issue the USD.

Although the US is very slowly losing its status as the global financial superpower, all major commodities are traded in USD, countries keep their foreign reserves in USD, and most international debt obligations are met in USD. This provides the dollar with an unparalleled demand globally for the moment, especially for non-US investors. These reasons make the USD a great currency diversifier.

USD Performance

The most effective way to measure the USD's performance is by using the US Dollar Index (DXY). It is a measurement of how the USD has performed against a basket of different currencies instead of a single currency. Below is the lifetime chart of the DXY.

Source: Marketwatch

The USDX was at 79.335 on the 1st of January 2010, and it was at 97.296 on the 1st of January 2020. The USDX shows a remarkable increase of 17.961 or 22.6% in the USD's strength against the major currencies of the world. Keeping in mind that this is the performance of the US dollar against other strong currencies such as the Euro, Japanese yen, and British pound. If the currency you have used to purchase the USD is not a primary world currency, the chances are that not only will you be soundly protected against the risks of inflation; you will experience an overall appreciation even after adjusting for inflation. The USD is an excellent hedge against inflation, especially for non-US investors.

Let's suppose you're an investor located in the US. In that case, however, it's better to diversify your non-US currency exposure as there is some long-term risk to the US Dollar due to political instability, humongous trade deficit, and debt.

How to invest in the United States Dollar?

You can invest in the USD by buying it directly from money exchanges. You can also buy it on various online investing platforms as a pair with another currency. Another way to invest in USD is by investing in a USD-focused ETF such as an ETF that tracks the USD's performance against six major currencies. The US dollar is one of the most focused currencies in speculative circles. You can invest in it by way of futures and options where you will profit if the price changes in your favor.

Japanese Yen

The Japanese yen has also held its position firmly as a safe haven currency for the last two decades. There are several reasons for this. One reason is that Japan has remained the top creditor nation in the world for a long time, which means that Japan always holds a considerable portfolio of debt issued by other countries. When economic uncertainty seeps into the markets, Japan starts selling these debt instruments. The buyers have to purchase the debt in yen, and as a result, the yen experiences a surge in demand and gets stronger while other currencies get weaker. Another reason that keeps the Yen stable is that Japan is an attractive market for raising finance due to its near-zero interest rates. Since the debt obligations are met in the yen, the demand for the yen always remains high.

Japanese Yen Performance

An interesting dataset that can instantly paint a clear picture of the Japanese Yen's performance is its trend against major currencies since the start of the pandemic in 2020. While other currencies got weaker because they were issuing more debt to support their economies, the Yen registered incredible strength against both the US dollar and the British pound. The JPY/USD rate in early March was 110, and the rate in December of the same year was 105. An incredible increase of about 5% during a global pandemic. It indeed remains a credible and secure safe haven to hedge against inflation.

Historically, we see that the Japanese yen has strengthened a lot in the last 30-40 years. A high volume of Japanese exports and their population's considerable savings rate is the main reason for its strength.

Japanese Yen currency is an ideal diversifier for people in the United States.

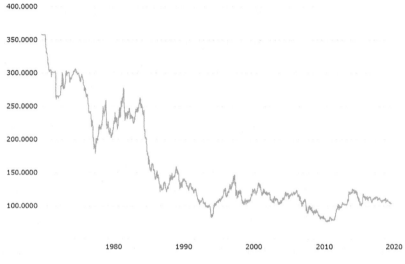

Source: Macrotrends

How to invest in the Japanese Yen?

The Japanese Yen follows the same path for investment options as other safe-haven currencies. Buying the currency from Forex markets in cash is one of the easiest ways to acquire the currency and build your portfolio. The Japanese yen is also a focus of various Exchange Traded Funds specializing in its nature as a safe haven currency. Investing in these ETFs might be a more suitable option if you do not prefer owning the currency itself. If you want to invest by way of speculation, the Yen allows for an abundance of investment in the options and futures markets. However, these come attached with more risks than ETFs and cash holdings.

Swiss Franc

The Swiss Franc is a strong safe haven currency, mostly because of Switzerland's stability over many centuries. The country remains politically neutral, which adds to the strength of its currency. The Swiss National Bank adopts a policy of zero inflation which results in the franc not losing any value. Because of these reasons, the Swiss Franc appreciates in times of economic uncertainty and thus continues to be valued as a safe haven currency globally.

Because the Swiss Franc enjoys immense popularity amongst investors, it is consistently in high demand. This demand keeps pushing the Swiss Franc value higher and trades on all major Forex markets. Its code is CHF. It mostly trades as a pair with the United States dollar, the Euro, and the British pounds in codes USD/CHF, EUR/CHF, and GBP/CHF.

Swiss Franc Performance

The Swiss Franc continues to enjoy its status as a safe haven alongside the Japanese yen. Historical data shows that the Franc has consistently appreciated against the US dollar for a better part of the last two decades. You could buy 1 USD for roughly 1 Swiss Franc in the middle of 2010, whereas currently, you need 0.9 Swiss francs to purchase 1 USD. Even though this may seem like a small appreciation in value for ten years, it is essential to keep in mind that we base this appreciation against the all-powerful United States dollar, which itself is a stable currency. So, if the Swiss franc appreciates against the USD, it will certainly protect your financial position against any risks that inflation poses. Historically, we see that the Swiss Franc is powerful against the US dollar and that the Swiss Franc has strengthened significantly over the last 20 years.

Switzerland is a stable non-EU country with neutral politics and is very business-friendly.

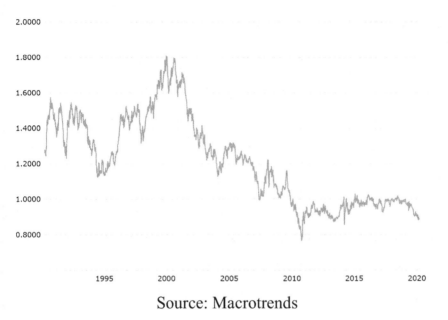

Source: Macrotrends

How to invest in the Swiss Franc?

The easiest way would be to buy Swiss francs from currency exchanges. The next best option would be to buy Swiss francs as pairs in the online forex markets. Various online platforms allow you to do this. As with all other currencies discussed above, Swiss Franc focused ETFs are an excellent investment if you don't want to buy the currency on its own. You also have the option of investing in Swiss franc futures and options. Be advised, though, that futures and options are speculative instruments and are riskier than owning the currency independently.

Thai Baht

Thailand has experienced an explosion in tourism in recent times. The government has invested heavily in making the country an ideal tourist destination for people worldwide. It is popular amongst European travelers looking to get away from their cold and rainy weather to the warm beaches of Thailand. What this translates to is a high demand for the Thai Baht. When demand for a currency is more elevated, its value usually goes up. Thailand has also consistently posted a trade surplus for a better part of the last decade, which has enabled the Thai Baht to appreciate significantly in value throughout the same time frame.

Thai Baht Performance

The currency has appreciated against the USD, the Euro, the GBP, and many other major world currencies in the last decade. Very few currencies have shown such a performance against a large basket of world currencies, which makes the Thai Baht an excellent investment for US-based investors.

We can see this in the 20-year historical chart for the Thai Baht against the USD below.

The primary reason for this is due to the increased tourism from Western countries to Thailand.

The Thai Baht is an excellent diversifier as it doesn't follow the charts of other Western countries. However, as with all diversifiers, do not invest too much in it.

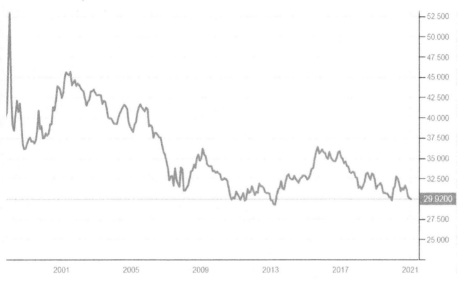

How to invest in the Thai Baht?

The Thai Baht trades in similar ways to the other currencies we have talked about above. The easiest way is to purchase the currencies from online or in-store exchanges. Like other similar currencies, many ETFs focus on the Thai Baht as a core investment and take precautions to offset any abrupt volatility. These are safer than buying the currency in cash.

A Short message from the Author:

Hey, are you enjoying the book? I'd love to hear your thoughts!

Many readers do not know how hard reviews are to come by, and how much they help an author.

I would be incredibly thankful if you could take just 60 seconds to write a brief review on Amazon, even if it's just a few sentences!

Thank you for taking the time to share your thoughts!

Your review will genuinely make a difference for me and help gain exposure for my work.

Real Estate

Real Estate is a lucrative alternative to stocks that offers lower risk and higher returns on investment. It can be a desirable investment as a tangible asset that can be controlled. Most commonly, real estate investments materialize returns through rent from properties, which provide a constant source of income. Profits can also be made through appreciation, as property can be sold after its value goes up beyond the cost of investment. For long-term investments, real estate can be leveraged to expand your holdings.

The passive, stable income earned from real estate is one of the significant benefits of this investment. Such an income can cover monthly expenses and make a profit while allowing investment in several properties, which mitigates risk. This also provides investors with long-term financial stability, as properties appreciate over time. Real estate is also a sought-after investment in periods of high inflation, as the property value increases with inflation, acting as a hedge against it. All in all, it is a good source of sustained cash flow and profits.

Below is a chart of median housing prices in the US over the last 100 years. The dip around 2008 is due to the housing credit crisis. In general, we see that housing prices tend to track inflation.

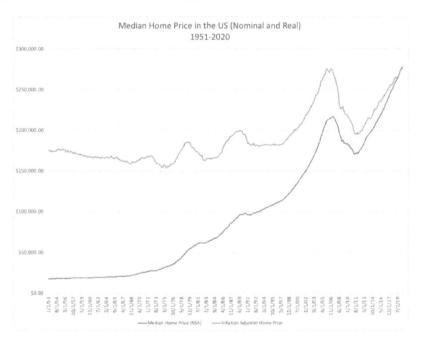

Source: DQYDJ, www.dqydj.com

How to identify real estate markets with good cash flow and low debt?

Real estate with good cash flow and low debt can translate not only into profits but also allow further investment in other properties. For this reason, it is vital to identify markets that expound on this benefit to get the most out of real estate investment. The process of identifying profitable real estate markets requires a lot of research. This should involve analyzing market performance through research reports and newspaper articles, particularly relating to properties you might be interested in. You should also keep an eye on microeconomic factors that shape each market, including job growth, housing prices, rental rates, construction starts, and supply and demand forces. All of these factors determine the growth and value of a market and indicate the sort of returns that can be expected in the future.

Additionally, capitalization rate or cap rate calculations come in handy when deciding on real estate investments. Cap rates are determined by dividing a property's net operating income by the current market value and reflect an estimation of potential returns on a real estate investment. This formula can provide a look into the initial yield of an investment property and can aid the decision-making process to maximize profits.

Additional calculations that can help appraise potential investments include price-to-rent ratios, which compare median home prices with median rent, and can determine likely demand for rental properties, which in turn predicts rising value.

An excellent way to value real estate is by using the RV ratio. The RV ratio is the Rent-to-Value ratio which determines the percentage of a month's rent of a property to the total purchase price of the property. For example, a house that costs $200,000 to purchase and has a monthly rent of $1,000 has an RV ratio of 0.5%. An ideal RV ratio is above 0.7%. So, for the same house, if the purchase price remains the same at $200,000, and if the rental yield rises to $2000, this would produce an RV ratio of 1%, which is ideal.

Net Operating Income (NOI) analyses the profitability of income-generating investments, giving an estimation of a property's value. Some other key factors that can indicate good cash flow properties include a diversified economy with a rapidly growing job market and population growth, as well as increasing demand for rental properties and commercial spaces. You should also identify affordable property prices, as high investment costs can reduce net cash flow.

Residential Real Estate

Residential real estate includes all properties intended for living. This includes everything from single-family houses to multi-family residences. Housing being a necessity, residential real estate is less sensitive to economic conditions. This has made it a common investment choice, especially for the long-term.

Why does Residential Real Estate have value?

Globally, median house prices increased by 6.9% in 2019 and continue to grow at a rate of 1.9% in 2020. Historically, home prices have risen with inflation rates as the cost of materials increases. House prices are also subject to market forces, which leads to a higher value with increased demand. This often comes from urbanization, the advent of nuclear families and independent living, as well as the rise of the middle-class. Residential real estate is therefore viewed as a safe investment with guaranteed returns.

How effective is Residential Real Estate against inflation?

In recent housing bubbles, house prices have increased faster than inflation rates. With such trends, residential real estate is seen as an effective hedge against inflation, especially in the long run. In addition, as home mortgages come with lower interest rates, residential real estate increases in value while monthly payments remain stable, effectively countering the effects of inflation.

How can you invest in Residential Real Estate?

Owning rental properties can provide a regular income if they are rented while the property appreciates. Mortgaged ownership of rental properties is an investment that hedges against inflation. You can also invest in Real Estate Investment Groups (REIGs). REIGs operate by allowing investors to buy into a company that buys or builds residential apartments.

You can also flip houses by buying a home and increasing its value with specific repairs and updates before selling at a profit. Alternatively, homes can be purchased in a rapidly rising market and sold for a profit. To diversify your real estate portfolio, you can also invest in Real Estate Limited Partnerships (RELPs). RELPs buy and hold a variety of properties and make profits once the property is sold.

Real Estate Materials Retailers

Real estate materials companies are involved in the production and sale of building materials, home improvement products, and services, as well as rental tools and equipment. They also offer long-term commercial contracts. Materials companies' value and performance are inherently linked to that of real estate. With relatively stable demand, materials companies usually operate with high returns and profits for investors.

Why are Real Estate Materials Retailers suitable investments?

Real estate materials companies derive their value from the inherent link to real estate and property development. As the value of developed property and real estate increases, so does that of materials companies that provide building, improvement, and maintenance materials. Not only that, but demand for materials companies is also directly tied to demand for real estate. While they can be more dependent on market forces, materials companies can be counted on to offer returns on investment.

How effective are Real Estate Materials Retailers against inflation?

Inflationary periods mark an increase in the value of real estate. This increase also translates significantly to real estate materials companies, providing a sufficient hedge against sudden inflation hikes. Even when real estate values, like house values, drop due to lower purchasing power that lowers demand, demand for home improvement and maintenance remains relatively stable. Long-term commercial contracts do not respond quickly to inflation when signed before inflationary hikes, so they stay relatively stable in the face of rising inflation rates.

How can you invest in Real Estate Materials Retailers?

Real estate development companies that trade publicly can be invested in by buying shares on the stock market. Increasing dividends overtime provides higher cash flow to investors. Investment risk can also be diversified by investing in stocks from different companies. Some of the largest real estate materials companies include *Home Depot* and *Lowes*, the former holding 47% of the market share in the US and steadily growing. Suitable investments can be made in such companies by first identifying those with good cash flow, high returns, and risk mitigation strategies.

Real Estate Development Companies

Real estate development companies are involved in activities ranging from renovation and re-lease of existing properties to buying and selling of raw land, as well as the sale of developed lands. Developers are involved in the creation and renovation of real estate, and these processes can determine the value of the resulting property. Real estate investors often work closely with developers to increase their returns.

Why are Real Estate Development Companies suitable investments?

When a property is developed, its value increases. The appeal of property development, therefore, lies in the potentially higher operating profits and capital gains upon sale of a property. Real estate development responds to market forces, that is, it increases with demand and can guarantee returns and even increase the value of surrounding commercial and residential real estate. As demand for residential and commercial real estate is inherently linked, real estate development companies can ensure high returns on investment in property development.

How effective are Real Estate Development Companies against inflation?

Real estate development companies are expected to grow in inflationary periods. This growth can be attributed to the lower purchasing power of money during inflation, which leads to higher prices translating to higher earnings from development. As the cost of building materials is higher, the property value also increases. Especially in areas where there is a certainty of demand, development companies can offer a good hedge against inflation. Dividends from shares also grow in time and provide higher cash flows to investors, even with rising inflation rates.

How can you invest in Real Estate Development Companies?

You can invest in real estate development companies by buying stocks of publicly trading companies on the stock exchange, based on the company's performance and annual returns. You can also make long-term investments by raising capital for development projects, where you can earn a share of the profits from the sale of developed lands. Alternatively, investors can also offer loans to development companies to finance their projects and make profits on the interest paid on the loan.

Real Estate Investment Trusts (REITs)

Real Estate Investment Trusts (REITs) are formed when a corporation utilizes investor money to buy, operate and manage income properties. REITs are not subject to corporate tax, as they pay out about 90% of their income as dividends. REITs dabble in equity and mortgage-backed securities offering diversified exposure to real estate, as they allow indirect investment in commercial, residential, and industrial real estate. They are best for investors who wish to add real estate to their portfolios without traditional transactions.

Why are Real Estate Investment Trusts suitable investments?

REITs operate much like mutual funds but allow a lot more control over where your money goes. They enable investors entry into non-residential assets, which can be otherwise difficult for individual investors. As they are exchange-traded, REITs are also highly liquid, allowing faster cash transfers. They offer investors regular income, as well as opportunities for appreciation. REITs are also mostly affordable for individual investors. With pooled capital, they are able to invest in tremendous assets.

How useful are Real Estate Investment Trusts against inflation?

Over the past 25 years, REITs have experienced consistently growing dividends at almost twice the inflation rate. REITs provide natural protection against inflation. Their value is derived from real estate value, which increases with inflation. This allows for REIT dividend growth and provides a stable source of income throughout inflationary periods. REITs also mainly diversify risk, as they own a multi-property portfolio that remains relatively stable even if one asset reduces in value due to inflation.

How can you invest in Real Estate Investment Trusts?

Publicly traded REITs are listed on the stock exchange, and shares can be bought and sold through a broker. Alternatively, you can invest in REIT mutual funds, which themselves invest in REITs, and their share prices are not subject to fluctuation. ETFs are also available for REITs, which support the majority of their assets in equity REIT securities. They incur lower investment costs on higher returns and offer trading flexibility through diversification and risk management.

Cash Flow

Cash flow refers to the incoming and outgoing finances of a business. The cash coming into a business is primarily the earnings of the company. These earnings depend on what the business is focused on. Some businesses may earn through the service they provide, whereas others may rely on goods they sell. The outgoing cash is essentially the expenditure that the company has. Similar to the incoming cash, this too can be attributed to several different aspects. The salary paid to the employees, the liabilities, any bills or additional expenses, and the production costs (if a product is being produced) all contribute to cash exiting the business.

The cash that the business actually benefits from is the difference that gets left behind when the expenditures are subtracted from the incoming money. As a result of inflation, it is usually this different that is affected the most, and thus the entire cash flow is impacted.

Nominal Cash Flow vs. Real Cash Flow

The cash flow of a business that is calculated without considering the influence of inflation in the future is referred to as nominal cash flow. On the other hand, real cash flow is the cash flow estimated considering the effects of inflation. The latter then becomes a good way for comparing the current cash flow to that of the past. A high inflation rate causes the real cash flow to be a lot less than the nominal cash flow.

Why are high cash flow producing businesses a good investment?

A high positive cash flow implies that the business has more significant finances to support the business activities. It is when the profits earned by the business outweigh the expenditures. Investing in such a business yields higher chances of receiving more incredible and more profitable returns. A business that is already flourishing would get the opportunity of expanding even further with additional investment. Expansion of goods or services would directly correlate to catering to a greater audience and, subsequently, increased sales. Investment in a business that focuses on processing raw materials is an incredibly profitable idea. Extra funds would imply that the company has the facility of buying and storing more raw materials to process and utilize later. This would help save the business from suffering because of the price hikes of raw materials.

How can positive cash flows hedge against inflation?

As aforementioned, a positive cash flow means that the business is earning more than it is spending. This difference can be positively impacted by the additional investment made and negatively affected by external conditions such as the market inflation. During inflation, a business increases the prices of the product or service it offers its consumers. However, at the same time, the firm also has to sustain an increase in the production costs, and labor costs.

The greater the cash flow, the lower the business is impacted by the inflation rates. This is because the substantial earnings allow the company to recover any costs lost to the high inflation rate. Generally, if a business has a return rate of greater than 5%, it's stable enough to sustain the effects of regular inflation. A positive cash flow further allows a business to spend on other profitable investments that we have covered such as commodities and assets.

A business with a positive cash flow can raise its prices to maintain its real cash flow during high inflationary periods.

RV Rental Business (Renting out RV's)

The RV rental business revolves around customers renting RVs to travel and live in them. There are many different types of RVs that can be rented out in a RV rental business; including caravans, motorhomes, and campervans. Many people prefer to rent RVs whilst on a trip to cut down costs and to experience living outdoors.

Why is an RV Rental Business a good investment?

RVs are a highly sought-after option for investment. This is because they prove to be cheaper than hotels and allow savings to be made in the transportation costs. Keeping this in mind, investing in a RV business timely can help you obtain high returns.

How effective is a RV Rental Business against inflation?

RV rental businesses create cash flow by the rental fees paid by the customers. The maintenance costs along with any other expenses are deducted from this fee to determine whether the cash flow is positive or negative.

The business owner has the prerogative to increase this rental fee during inflation as the maintenance costs increase too. This makes the RV rental business to be highly effective against inflation. If a positive cash flow is created, this surplus can then be invested to buy or lease more RVs to rent out. The existing RVs can also be upgraded. In short, even during inflation, investments can be made that will contribute to creating more positive cash flow in the RV rental business. Some customers may even prefer to rent RVs for a longer period. Even though some discounts may be offered in such a circumstance, the business still benefits from the continuous rental fee of the RV.

How can you set up or invest in a RV Rental Business?

Setting up an RV business does not require any specialized skill. Rather, with a few simple steps, you can kick-start your business to start building cash flow. The main things you need to focus on is setting a suitable rental fee for the RVs and managing the costs. The primary costs your RV rental business will have would be the upkeep and maintenance costs of the RVs. These can include oil changes, tyre changing, and ensuring overall cleanliness. Another expenditure could also be the advertisement costs that you would have to pay. An initial cost that you will also have to bear would involve buying or leasing different RVs.

Online Apparel Store

Online shopping has always been profitable not only for the customers but even more so for the investors. They provide customers the facility of shopping a wide range of clothing whilst sitting within the comforts of their home. Buyers can browse and choose whichever piece of clothing they desire, check sizes, and then get the order delivered all through a few clicks.

Why is an Online Apparel Store a good investment?

One of the biggest reasons why a lot of customers are turning towards online shopping is the convenience it provides. It saves the buyers the hassle of traveling time to the store and allows them to save time by providing perks such as express delivery. Online apparel stores have become even more popular during the current pandemic situation. Customers can easily choose what they wish to buy, place an order, and get the clothes delivered at home, without any human interaction.

How effective is an Online Apparel Store against inflation?

An online apparel store is one of the easier business to create positive cash flow. This is because the investor reduces the expenditure that plays a significant role in traditional apparel stores. These include the costs of renting or buying the store location, the electricity bills, and hiring employees to help assist the walk-in customers amongst many others. Since these costs are absent for an online apparel store, the cash flow becomes positive thus helping an online apparel store prove to be highly effective during inflation. The biggest challenge is to ensure that the profit is higher than the advertising costs + manufacturing costs. Analysing your competition beforehand will help with this.

You can also expect to make a much higher profit if you source your merchandise from overseas. Countries like China, Bangladesh, India, Vietnam, and Thailand produce garments of an excellent quality and sell it for economical prices. This margin is itself a hedge against inflation particularly because you will always be able to find a vendor at your price point as their markets contain hundreds of suppliers.

The fact that during inflation the prices of the clothing being sold also increases add-ons to the creation of a positive cash flow. The most notable expenditure of an online apparel store, apart from the purchasing costs, is hiring a customer service team and building a website.

Since these expenditures are not directly impacted by inflation, the earnings made during the period outweigh the costs. This contributes to generating a positive cash flow even during the inflation period.

How can you set up or invest in an Online Apparel Store?

The most important part of setting up an online store is buying the services of a third-party website-creating platforms such as WordPress or Woocommerce. Your online apparel store will start operations as soon as the website is up and running. Another very important consideration is to ensure that there is enough stock to cater to a large number of orders in the business' inventory. This is where a positive cash flow becomes beneficial. With a great cash flow, an online apparel store can make certain that there is enough stock in the inventory to fulfil diverse orders from customers without making them wait.

The branding and advertising of the online apparel store is very crucial to deciding whether the business makes enough sales to create a positive cash flow. Advertising on social media platforms or collaborating with other already well-established businesses may help with achieving a decent amount of exposure to get your store going.

Online Aviation Merchandise Store

The aviation industry has mesmerized generations and has created an army of loyal enthusiasts. These people love everything about aviation and are willing to part easily with their hard-earned cash just to get closer to the industry. They spend hundreds of dollars individually on aviation related merchandise, aircraft models, and plane tags. https://aviationtravelshop.com/ is a popular aviation merchandise store in Australia.

Why is an Aviation Merchandise Store a good investment?

Aviation enthusiasts love to spend money on aviation merchandise and retailers leave no opportunity dry when they are designing products. For example, airplane tags are particularly popular among aviation fans. This is because these tags are made from real aircraft skin. This makes these tags very unique as they were once part of a magnificent machine that flew tens of thousands of miles over its lifetime. Fans of the industry also love buying aircraft models. Especially popular models are those of planes that are no longer in service such as the Airbus A380, the Concorde, and the Qantas 747. The industry fanbase is only growing by the day and demand for its merchandise will remain strong for the foreseeable future which makes an online store selling merchandise an excellent investment.

How effective is an Aviation Merchandise Store against inflation?

An online store that is running a successful sales strategy can be an extremely lucrative investment. The best part about this niche is that it targets a want-based audience. Most aviation enthusiasts understand that aviation merchandise does not come cheap which prepares them to shell out hundreds of dollars on individual plane models. The profit margins on these models are exceptionally high which greatly helps with driving up profits. Your online store can produce a healthy cash flow and provide you with a decent profit every month which will effectively shield you from any inflation induced worries.

How can you set up or invest in an Aviation Merchandise Store?

As with any online store, the first thing you need is the store itself. Ecommerce stores are easy to set up these days using popular platforms such as Shopify. Once you have the store set up, the next thing you would have to do is look for suppliers. Again, the internet is your friend. There are hundreds of suppliers out there for generic content but very free that sell official aircraft models and even fewer that sell original plane tags. This makes it very important to be extra careful when choosing your vendors. After your vendors have been finalised, you have to start selling your stock. Best areas to market your store are aviation related groups and pages on social media as well as by using paid ads on search engines.

Online Used Computer Parts Store

Since the turn of the century, almost every industry has become heavily dependent on computers. Almost all business transactions now involve the use of computers. With growing developments in data science and artificial intelligence, computers are extremely important now more than ever.

Why is a Used Computer Parts Store a good investment?

These advancements have also made new computers extremely expensive, making them unaffordable to a large majority of users. Instead of buying new computers, people are increasingly investing in used computers or choosing to repair their old computers to save costs. Setting up a used computer parts store, thus, becomes an excellent business investment. Considering that computer parts are not a perishable commodity, the risk of losses because of products being destroyed is reduced too.

How effective is a Used Computer Parts Store against inflation?

The used computer parts in the store can primarily come from two different sources. They can either be bought from private sellers who sell their computers part by part, or they can be repaired parts. Both ways, obtaining the parts does not add significantly to the expenses of setting up a computer parts business. However, in order to ensure that a positive cash flow is created, you need to make sure that other costs are also kept low. These include costs such as the rent of the store and the helping hands hired for the customers' assistance.

Used computer parts sell at a significant price and are subject to becoming more expensive as a result of inflation. This is because of reduced supply of parts for older computer models with the passage of time. This hike along with other factors contributes to making a used computer parts store an effective investment during inflation.

How can you set up or invest in a Used Computer Parts Store?

Setting up an online computer parts store should not be difficult given that there are so many online platforms that make it easy to do so. You can go with the standard Shopify route or you can go with the traditional WordPress path. The WordPress option will require you to use an eCommerce plugin such as WooCommerce or BigCommerce as described previously. Once you have the store up and running, you can start marketing it on computer parts related pages. Don't forget to mention that you check all parts for quality and performance before you sell them to increase confidence in your store as you are selling used items.

Good Debt Options

Good debt includes borrowing that can help build long-term wealth. With good debt, you can leverage the power of your money to create passive income streams that, over time, can build wealth. It is considered a sensible investment in one's financial future as it offers benefits that do not have a negative impact, unlike bad debt which drains wealth and is difficult to repay.

Why are good debt options a good investment?

While it might be a compelling idea to remain debt-free, it is almost impossible to do so without also forgoing lucrative investment opportunities that can build wealth in the future. Good debt options offer the opportunity to invest in the future in responsible yet rewarding ways that can improve your own net worth, give returns and improve the quality of life. Without good debt, investments in education or real estate, residential or commercial might not be possible. These can limit your opportunities in the future. Responsible management of debt can also improve credit scores, which can open doors for other investments.

In the short-term, good debt, like all borrowing, incurs monthly costs and can restrict cash flow. Over time, this investment can start to offer returns that not only cover the debt, but also translate into profits that can be further invested for gains. Investments in good debt can also keep you away from impulse borrowing that results in bad debt that can deplete your finances and make recovery difficult. Good debt comes with the guarantee that not only can it be paid back but can also offer returns in the future.

Long Term Property Finance

Long-term property financing refers to investments in real estate through borrowing. Long-term financing like mortgages is considered good debt, as they can offer higher returns on the investment when property values rise beyond the borrowed amount. Long-term financing is used for investments in property that will generate returns in the future. Mortgages are a common source of finance for residential real estate investments as well as commercial real estate as commercial real estate loans.

Why is Long Term Property Financing a good investment?

Long-term property financing offers several benefits to investors that make it a valuable investment. Long-term borrowing can come with low interest rates, as the property itself acts as a collateral to the loan. It also increases cash flow, when smaller amounts are being paid out on interest, and other sources of income and finance are open to cover expenses and be invested elsewhere. Payments on long-term loans are also designed based on investors capabilities on a regular basis, and these helps build credit for future borrowing. Additionally, long-term property financing is a lucrative investment based on the value of the underlying property, promising high returns.

How effective is Long Term Property Financing against inflation?

Inflationary periods are known to lead to increases in property value. For this reason, long-term property financing is not only a profitable investment, it can also hedge against inflation. Property that is bought before high inflationary periods with long-term loans will increase in value during times of high inflation, beyond the amount of investment. You will still be paying the same monthly instalments on your loan, but their value will fall. At this time, the property, be it residential or commercial, can even be sold so that it covers the borrowed amount and leaves a profit for the investor. Inflationary periods benefit borrowers by enabling them to pay off a debt that is worth less than it was at the time of borrowing.

For this to happen, you have to make sure that the debt on the property is **a long-term fixed rate mortgage**. If the debt is variable rate, then you run the risk of increasing interest rates with inflation.

How can you invest in Long Term Property Financing?

A common source of long-term property financing is mortgages. Also known as home loans, they allow individuals to invest in residential real estate as a long-term investment. Mortgages hold the property being bought as collateral with monthly instalments. Mortgages can also be taken out for commercial real estate, although these differ slightly in amortization periods and interest rates. A purchase-money mortgage can also be taken out, where loans are financed by the property seller. Once a balloon payment has been made, you can keep this source of finance or refinance with a traditional lender.

Hot Money Investments

Hot money involves the flow of funds from one country to another for short-term profits on interest rates or anticipated exchange rate shifts. Such investments are referred to as hot money because they can move very quickly in and out of markets. Hot money investments can occur locally, by investing in short-term certificates of deposit with unusually high interest rates. Internationally, foreign investors can move their money to different countries to take advantage of higher interest rates that combat local inflation rates. Foreign investors buy securities from emerging markets.

To make this investment, make sure that you have good knowledge of the foreign marketing that you are investing into. Preferably you are working with reliable locals in that market; or actually living there.

Why is Hot Money a good investment?

Hot money indicates currencies that can quickly move between financial markets, and ensure investors are able to benefit from the highest short-term interest rates available. As a short-term investment, hot money regularly yields quick high returns on investment as it moves from low interest rate countries to those with higher interest rates. Such investments diversify risk by expanding portfolios. It also counters lower returns in local markets due to low interest rates so that the same investment can make higher earnings in international markets.

How effective is Hot Money Investment against inflation?

Investments are typically made in foreign countries experiencing higher inflation rates than local markets. In high inflationary periods, interest rates increase. This is the optimal time to make hot money investments as rates continue to rise in foreign markets. Hot money investments benefit from high inflation rates commonly found during inflationary periods. An example of a productive hot money investment can be found in the 10% earning made by Swiss investors when they invested out of Swiss markets with -0.75% interest rates in Indian bonds at an interest rate of 9.25%. With government promises to stabilise exchange rates within 2% fluctuation, investors still made a 10% return in USD. Because the Government maintained a stable exchange rate of the INR to the USD for a full financial year, investors materialised gains in USD.

How can you invest in Hot Money?

Investing in hot money requires extensive market research and knowledge, as well as financial acumen. Such investments can be made in foreign countries with higher inflation rates compared to local markets, to maximize returns. Making hot money investments with short-term portfolio investments, including bonds, equities, and financial derivatives. You can also invest in short-term foreign bank loans, and foreign bank loans with short-term investment horizons. You should keep in mind that hot money investments do not work over the long-term and are not suited to those who are not willing to move markets quickly, as returns can only be made during a limited period of time.

Refinancing of Existing Property

Refinancing involves the replacement of an existing debt obligation with another debt obligation under new terms. With refinancing, the previous debt is paid off, leaving only the new debt to be paid on agreed conditions. This is done for a variety of reasons, including availing better instalment conditions or lower interest rates. A common type of property refinancing is mortgage refinancing on houses, usually to get a loan that better fits the homeowner's financial situation. Refinancing existing property is a good debt that also offers cashouts.

Why is Refinancing Existing Property a good investment?

Refinancing holds value as an investment for several reasons. It offers lower interest rates compared to the previous loan, which not only saves money, but can speed up the rate at which equity is built. It could also potentially decrease monthly instalments, thereby improving cash flow. This can also significantly shorten the loan's term without increasing monthly payments. Refinancing can also reduce the risk associated with the debt, especially if switching from variable-rate to a fixed-rate loan. Finally, you can consolidate various other debts under one through refinancing, which can provide reduced monthly payments and short-term relief.

How effective is Refinancing Existing Property against inflation?

Refinance activities have seen an increase north of 65% in 2020 in the U.S. As inflation causes interest rates to rise, refinancing to a fixed-rate loan can offer a hedge against inflation. Fixed-rate loans charge a specified interest rate that does not fluctuate with inflation. Essentially, with such a loan, you can pay the same amount of money, but it now has less value. Not only is money saved on such a loan during inflationary periods, it can also make monthly payments easier to meet. Refinancing can also be used to cash-out on real estate properties that have increased in value during inflationary periods. This allows access to a higher loan amount while maintaining ownership.

How can you invest in Refinancing?

There are many ways to refinance your property to a beneficial outcome. The most common is rate-and-term refinancing, where a new loan agreement replaces the original loan with lower interest. This is often applied to mortgages. Cash-out refinancing can be used where cash is needed, against real estate that has increased in value. This way you are able to gain the value of the property without selling it. Cash-in refinancing can be used to pay down a portion of the loan for smaller loan payments, which can improve cash flow. Alternatively, consolidation refinancing is used to pay off several debts with one new loan, which decreases monthly payments and increases cash flow.

Refinancing is best done when long term interest rates have been lowered significantly since you started your mortgage payments. A good time would be when the interest rates have been lowered due to a recession and you have the option to refinance at lower rates.

Inflation-Indexed Bonds

Inflation-indexed bonds or securities are produced to offer investors a safe and risk-free option to protect their portfolios against inflation. These securities are primarily issued by sovereign governments. They are designed to offset the loss in purchasing power of a currency by giving returns that either match or outperform the expected inflation levels of an economy. These are also referred to as real securities. This is because their returns are meant to offer profits that are usually adjusted for inflation. They are meant to protect your liquidity by ensuring a return that either beats or matches the negative effects inflation would otherwise have.

Also keep in mind that Inflation indexed bonds are not particularly great investment vehicles if you are looking for higher returns. This is because other asset classes such as gold and some currencies not only protect you from inflation but also vastly outperform it. As with all government securities, their rates of return are fixed and therefore you know exactly how much you will stand to make after a certain period. But the main difference with inflation adjusted bonds is that their principal changes during their life. This is how the bonds can offer protection against inflation. There are different methods used by different issuing authorities which determine how the principal changes.

For example, one issuer might choose to change the principal value of a bond by adjusting with the CPI on a semi-annually basis. So, a 10-year $10,000 bond with a fixed 2% rate will accrue $100 during the first six months. If the prevalent CPI has a figure of 3%, the principal value of the bond will increase by $150 after six months which will take the value of the principal to $10,150. The bond will accrue interest for the second six-month period on the new principal value. So instead of 100$ before, the new interest value would be $101.5. This will ensure that the bond will adjust with the CPI to account for all effects of inflation. At the end of the maturity period, the holder of the bond will receive all the interest that has been accrued on the inflation adjusted principal. The bond holder will also receive the adjusted principal value.

Why are inflation indexed bonds a good investment?

These bonds come with a unique feature which is that their principal gets adjusted for inflation. This contrasts with other inflation adjusted bonds which have variable interest rates that change as a response to changes in inflation. The benefit with getting principal adjusted is that if the economy happens to undergo a period of high inflation period at the beginning of the bond's lifetime, its principal will get adjusted to a fairly high value. Going forward, if inflation reduces over time and the economy does not experience near 0 inflation or deflation, then even with moderate interest rates that were fixed when the security was issued, the bond will yield a much higher return due to the high principal value.

For example, a 20-year $10,000 bond that has a 2% rate is issued with semi-annual adjustment. The economy registers a CPI of 7% for 2 and a half years, 5% for the next 2 and a half years, and 3% for the remaining 15 years. The bond would accrue $100 for the first six months. The principal would increase by $350 and the interest value would increase by $3.5. The principal would continue to increase by 7% p.a for the next 2 years compounded semi-annually. It would then increase by 5% p.a for the next 2 and a half years compounded annually. After five years, the principal will have a value of $12,983. You would earn interest for the new principal every time the interest gets accrued, which is semi-annually in this case. So, the interest value at the start of the 6th year would be $129.83 instead of the $100 that was accrued at the very start. This value would only increase as the 2% CPI would still cause principal adjustment for the remaining 15 years of the bond even with a 2% interest rate.

Inflation-Indexed Bonds performance against inflation

Inflation-indexed bonds are excellent investment vehicles against inflation. As inflation is usually measured by the CPI, and since these bonds get their principal adjusted according to the changing CPI, they produce returns that more or less beat inflation over a long term. However, this is only true when an economy does not experience deflation as the principal can also be adjusted to a lower value if the value of CPI becomes negative. Historically, with the exception of the deflation period experienced by the US economy between the end of 2007 and the middle of 2009, inflation-indexed bonds have consistently performed on par with their expectations.

How to invest in Inflation-Indexed Bonds

A sound way to invest in inflation-indexed bonds is by investing in Exchange Traded Funds that focus on similar securities. This is because these ETFs hold inflation-indexed bonds of different values, tenures, and maturities. They could be holding a 30-year $10,000 bond that mature next year, or a 10-year $5,000 bond that was issued last year. This has the potential to provide considerable protection against certain risks that you might otherwise be exposed to if you outright bought the security.

This is not to say that buying securities on their own is considerably worse. You can always invest directly in these securities by buying them from your local broker or bank.

Prime examples of top performing Inflation-Indexed Bonds

For investors who are particularly interested in investing in USD based investment, the Treasury Inflation-Protected Securities (TIPS) are an ideal choice. These bonds are issued in USD, they are linked with the US CPI, and in periods of inflation in the US economy, their principal also adjusts resulting in higher long-term

USD return. These can be especially popular for investors whose local currencies have historically performed poorly against the USD.

One of the top performing ETFs that is focused on inflation-indexed bonds is the PIMCO 15+ Year U.S. TIPS Index Exchange-Traded Fund (LTPZ) which has appreciated by an impressive 23.98% since the start of 2020. This return far outpaces major inflation levels throughout the world. Over the past 11 years, the fund has produced an average year-on-year return of 8%.

Stocks

Stocks are shares of companies that you can buy any number of to take ownership of a company. You can buy shares of any company, whether private or public, but for the purposes of this text, we will be talking about stocks of publicly traded companies.

A publicly traded company is a company that has some or all of its shares listed on a stock exchange and made available for sale and purchase by the public. Any member of the public can own a share in any publicly listed company. The number of shares you purchase determines how much of a company you own. Some shares of companies allow you to vote on major matters of the company such as the appointment of directors.

There are two ways through which you can monetarily benefit from owning stock of a company. The first is the appreciation in the value of the stock you hold, and the other are the dividends a company pays to shareholders. Both can be used to protect yourself against inflation. However, most companies that pay dividends usually start performing poorly in times of inflation. This is because their cost of production rises. Some companies can pass on that increase in cost to their consumers, while others cannot. This increase in prices of raw materials for example, can affect the ability of a company to keep paying dividends due to lower profits. This makes the value of the raw material stock the better option to consider when choosing a company to invest in to guard against inflation. Dividends are also sometimes not paid for other reasons that are not connected to inflation. The historical performance of a stock paints a clear enough picture for investors to help them make the correct choice regarding their investments.

How do stocks perform against inflation?

Since there are literally thousands of stocks to choose from to perform this analysis. It is hard to generalise how stocks perform against inflation. This is also difficult because stocks in one country might perform exceptionally well for an investor in another country. This could be due to fundamentals supporting the stock's performance or it could simply be the exchange rate that provides a better return for the investor.

However, a better way to judge how stocks perform against inflation is to not look at them individually. We will see later that the best way to invest in stocks is by investing in ETFs or index funds. This is because these assets contain a pool of diverse stocks from different companies. This allows them to protect their positions against volatilities in the stock price of any one company. Historically, both the S&P and the Dow Jones Industrial Average have returned positive inflation adjusted figures on average. We will discuss them in detail in a later section of this chapter.

It is worth noting that stocks have become very speculative these days. Although this does not apply to mature companies such as Coca Cola, it applies to almost major tech companies. And even though these companies tend to produce exceptionally high returns, they can also experience extremely high volatility in their stock price. We will explore tech stocks in detail but one thing to remember here is that tech stock performance is not a measurement of how stocks generally perform against inflation.

How to choose the right company to invest in

It really is the question of the hour. With thousands of companies listed on exchanges around the world, it becomes very difficult to pick and choose the correct stock to act as a hedge against inflation. However, this is made easier if we simply follow the fundamentals of inflation.

For example, since inflation causes a rise in prices of **consumer goods**, companies that are related to this sector will fare much better than others. This is also especially true for companies that can pass on the increase in prices of their raw materials directly onto consumers. Examples of such companies included food producers, oil and gas or energy companies, utility companies, and healthcare, etc.

ETFs, S&P 500, and the Dow Jones Industrial Average

But individual stocks do come with various risks. One major risk is that the corporation can experience a setback from a lot of different sources. This can be a new competitor, change in regulation that governs the company's target market, a corporate scandal, or loss in the company's leadership by the shareholders. All of these are extremely difficult to predict from the historical data that shows the performance of a company's stock. A much better way to invest in stocks is by investing in ETFs that have been designed to protect investors against inflation or those that mimic the most popular index funds such as the Standard & Poor 500 and the Dow Jones Industrial Average.

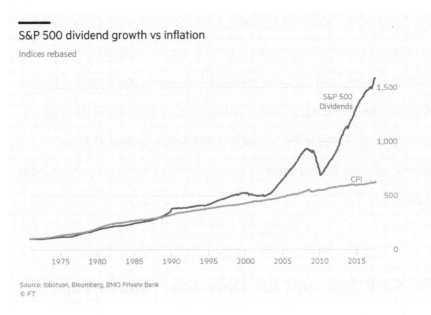

S&P 500 dividend growth vs inflation

Indices rebased

S&P 500 Dividends

CPI

1,500

1,000

500

0

1975 1980 1985 1990 1995 2000 2005 2010 2015

Source: Ibbotson, Bloomberg, BMO Private Bank
© FT

Source: https://www.pinterest.com/pin/497366352591275920/

https://i.pinimg.com/originals/6a/dc/1a/6adc1ab36d291cf60e93b0
db7b5049b3.jpg

The graph above shows that the S&P 500 index has returned higher than the US CPI for a better part of three decades. This makes this index fund an extremely appropriate investment to protect yourself against inflation as not only does it provide a protection against the harmful effects of inflation, it generally also returns a profit on your investment.

Are tech stocks safe investments against inflation?

There is usually no problem with any specific industry in terms of a stock as an investment. Some tech stocks are excellent investments against inflation while others are not very fruitful. The distinction is between growth companies and value companies.

You will see examples of various tech stocks in the markets today that have lots of debt and no profits to show for their operations. These companies will have extremely high valuations and some analysts might even refer to them as overvalued. These companies leverage their tech association to lure in investors who are highly interested in the company's growth potential. And sometimes, these companies experience rapid appreciation in their stock prices.

However, a prime example of when this can go wrong is of WeWork. WeWork was valued in the tens of billions of dollars after receiving funding several times from SoftBank. However, in the end, the fundamentals of the company were so bad to investors that the much-hyped planned initial public offering of the company failed. There is always a possibility of this happening to highly speculative growth centered tech stocks.

But that does not mean that all tech stocks are unsuitable investments. A popular investment acronym is FAANG which stands for Facebook, Amazon, Apple, Netflix, and Google. It includes 4 of the 5 top tech companies in the United States that are showing great promise as suitable investments for protecting a portfolio against inflation.

It is important to do a fundamental cash flow analysis of the companies involved, so that you can pick out stocks that are profitable and would benefit from an inflationary period.

Cryptocurrencies

Cryptocurrencies have gained immense popularity in the past decade. They have been endorsed by central banks, global financial institutions, and even social media giants. Their popularity has been built on their distinct features and characteristics.

A cryptocurrency is a virtual currency that is essentially a software created by performing complex mathematical calculations as dictated by code. The process operates over a network that involves several computers located throughout the world and is protected by a technology known as blockchain. Because the currency is protected by digital cryptography, it is unique in the sense that it cannot be counterfeited or spent twice. A major reason for the rise in popularity of cryptocurrencies is that unlike all other currencies, cryptocurrencies are not issued by any central bank. This makes cryptocurrencies immune to any manipulation by sovereign governments or central banks. Cryptocurrencies are protected using blockchain technology in such a way that their transfers are possible directly between two pirates without the need of a third party. Transfers of cryptocurrencies take several minutes but they have extremely low costs.

Because of the way cryptocurrencies are designed, they are by nature scarce and each new mined coin takes more resources. These contribute to a steady increase in prices which investors have attributed to the possibility of using cryptocurrencies as a hedge against inflation.

Note: A cryptocurrency investment is extremely speculative, and it's not recommended to invest more than 0.5-1% of your portfolio in crypto.

Bitcoin as an Asset Class and an Investment

Bitcoins are a unique payment system and a form of a reward for a process known as mining, and is primarily used in the exchange of products, services, or currencies. Bitcoins are the pioneer of a decentralized peer-to-peer payment system with no third parties involved. Bitcoins were the first execution of a concept under the name of "cryptocurrency" that was speculated and surfaced over a cypherpunks mailing list in 1998. The proposed idea meant a new form of money using cryptography (rather than middlemen or a central authority) to administer its transactions and creations. The design was finally implemented in 2009 after the bitcoin software was applied as open-source code (OSS). Its popularity has grown in the past decade as developers continue to work on its development.

Bitcoins are owned by no central authority and are rather controlled by bitcoin users worldwide. Bitcoin development is limited to improving the technology without enabling a change in the bitcoin protocol. Users can use any version or software but to remain compatible with each other similar rules must be applied for a uniform crypto network.

The backend network of Bitcoins is much more complicated than how users view it as a mere computer program. It shares 'blockchain' technology, which is a public ledger. The ledger enables the user's computer to verify how viable each bitcoin is for every transaction that takes place. Digital signatures protect each Bitcoin transaction allowing users to use their Bitcoin addresses to exchange Bitcoins. Additionally, Bitcoin mining refers to the process that produces more bitcoins by solving a computational puzzle, rewarding the miner with bitcoins in return.

The electronic cash system is recognized as a standard representation of a cryptocurrency and happens to be the most popular digital currency. Bitcoins are used by individuals worldwide. In 2017 alone there were up to approximately 5.8 million cryptocurrency wallet users, of which a large fraction were bitcoin users, as per a research conducted by the University of Cambridge.

The value of Bitcoin consistently appreciates over the long term although it has experienced an exceptional level of volatility over the years. Bitcoins that could be purchased for $0.0008-$0.8$ per Bitcoin are now valued at $39,334.20 each (8th January 2021). Bitcoin gained its value due its rising demand and limited supply. The negative correlation between the supply and demand of bitcoins is what drives the price up. Over time Bitcoins have matured in the crypto industry, gaining the attention of investors as it is increasingly being looked upon as a credible derivative that can be used as a hedge against inflation.

Bitcoins possess the largest market capitalization of any cryptocurrency today. Most economists regard bitcoins as a top-performing asset class with the unique traits it holds. However, a consensus on the nature of bitcoins remains undecided.

With the growing popularity of bitcoins as well as the rise of their value due to limited supply, investors are more convinced than ever to own bitcoins. Investment decisions can strongly rely on bitcoins' nature, making it essential to establish a consensus on whether bitcoins represent a new asset class.

Bitcoins are now being regulated in various jurisdictions worldwide that comply with local and international laws and allow investors to purchase bitcoins through established exchanges or crypto platforms legally.

The return on bitcoins and the risk-reward associated with it requires conclusions drawn from statistical approaches. Bitcoins have shown an insignificant correlation with other asset class traits. It is not associated with regular stocks or commodities as it goes in the normal world.

Despite bitcoins being relatively new in the market, the returns consistently outsize the preceding year's figures since crypto had begun and are now seen increasingly as suitable hedge against inflation. Bitcoins are an ideal investment primarily due to their fixed supply that stores value and contains enough potential to appreciate in the long run. Investment banks and institutional investors are consistently piling into the use of cryptocurrencies.

Litecoin and Ethereum

Cryptocurrencies are not limited to the use of bitcoins. There are several other investment options that investors opt for depending on their trading style and bankroll. Some prominent alternatives to cryptocurrencies apart from bitcoins are Ethereum and Litecoin.

Ethereum

Ethereum is a software platform designed in 2015 to serve the purpose of supporting decentralized contracts and digital cash. With a market cap of $69,604,579,809 (1/10 the size of bitcoins), Ethereum is the closest alternative to bitcoins one can find.

It is speculated that Ethereum holds the potential to revolutionize data protection, the finance industry, and social media. It also claims to secure, codify, and trade anything. It has gained support from significant financial organizations such as Microsoft Azure and Amazon Web Services.

Litecoin

Another well-versed option in the crypto market is Litecoin, referred to as the silver to bitcoin's gold. Litecoin is an open-source and decentralized software that is a form of digital cash.

Litecoin transaction fees are relatively lower, considering it requires minimal resources. Litecoin also tops bitcoin with a processing speed that is four times faster, posing as an ideal option in terms of efficiency and costs.

The future of Litecoin depicts a potentially good investment for most investors and is regarded as a close call to bitcoins.

Historical Performance Against Inflation

In 2009 when the initial trading of bitcoins had begun, the digital cryptocurrency had undergone a lot of volatility. The fluctuations in price were seen in 2010 when the value of a single bitcoin rose from $0.0008 to $0.8. Since then, bitcoins have experienced significant crashes and rallies. Mt.Gox surfaced into a marketplace for bitcoins, having 150,000 bitcoins exchanged every day. However, due to its volatile nature and speculations for fraud the exchange was taken down in 2013. By 2020 Bitcoins were able to regain its losses which were previously incurred and possess a market cap of over $732 billion as of January 8th, 2020. It is now traded on numerous licensed and credible exchanges such as Kraken, Coinbase and Gemini.

Bitcoins are carefully designed with a deflationary approach, in addition to being a unit that stores value. It represents a similar gold standard creating opportunities for crypto users and investors to rise above the adverse effects of inflation.

Bitcoins are popular for their incredible potential to provide industries with protection against inflation and pose as an inflationary hedge, encouraging investors to own more bitcoins. Tycoon investors refer to bitcoins as the new gold for the 21 century and consider them as being naturally immune to the impacts of inflation.

The performance of bitcoins against the global pandemic tells us a lot about the potential of bitcoins against inflation. COVID-19 measures had led to the implementation of an inflationary monetary policy, which encouraged an aggressive supply. The lockdowns measures had given rise to key areas and food staples, largely affecting businesses worldwide (Similar to the 1970s when the USA encountered massive unemployment, which led to gold being the currency savior against inflation)

Bitcoin happens to be an ideal hedge against inflation in this scenario. Bitcoins possess a natural inflationary trait with a fixed 21 million bitcoin supply. This limit is what drives the value of bitcoins up and makes them immune to monetary inflation.

The supply shortage against the rising demand for bitcoins depicts an increase in the future per unit price which is gaining the attention of investors worldwide.

Prospects as a Hedge Against Inflation

The limited supply of bitcoins creates an inflation hedge, unique to other asset classes as it is immune to the changes of a political environment within a country. Investors that purchase bitcoins are not intending to contribute to a deflationary measure but are using it as a hedge against the consequences of inflation. However, despite the benefits cryptocurrencies are speculative and highly volatile. In the worst-case scenario, investors may even lose all their money rather than gaining anything.

Apart from inflation, bitcoins also pose as a hindrance against a disruptive law and order due to political instability. The prospects of bitcoins seek potential in preventing additional factors that can trigger more inflation.

Police states practicing seizure of private wealth and bank accounts closing due to unreliable governments can be minimized with bitcoins. Corrupted systems, export-protecting devaluations are namely few inflation triggers that bitcoins act as a hedge against.

Worst case scenario - Hyperinflation

We have already discussed inflation at length throughout this book. It is a reduction in the purchasing power of a currency. Hyperinflation is accelerated version of inflation. When the rate of inflation is exceedingly high, usually over 50%, an economy is considered to experience hyperinflation. It quickly erodes the purchasing power of a local currency, significantly raises prices for goods, and causes the value of savings to drop dramatically. It usually occurs in extenuating circumstances such as war or an abject failure of economic policy. Because the rate of inflation increases rapidly during times of hyperinflation, the rates are usually measured on a daily basis. These daily rates sometimes fall between 5% and 10%. When the monthly CPI goes over 50%, an economy experiences hyperinflation.

What causes hyperinflation?

Hyperinflation is usually caused by an excessive money supply or an extreme lack of confidence in a country's currency by its citizens and trading partners. The most common reason for hyperinflation is when a central bank starts printing excessive amounts of money for one reason or the other. This is usually a result of an economic depression. An economic depression is different to a recession in the sense that it lasts much longer, usually a couple of years. Because of this, the central bank decides to pump more money into the economy to stimulate economic activity to get out of depression. However, sometimes the rise in money supply is not met with a proportionate rise in economic output. Due to ensuing depression, businesses increase the prices of goods and services in order to remain profitable. These increases are met by purchases because people have the money to buy them. Because the central bank continues to print more money, consumers continue to purchase products with ever increasing prices. As a consequence, hyperinflation takes hold.

Another reason that causes hyperinflation is when a local population does have the same confidence in the value of a currency as before. When this happens, a constant low confidence environment spreads across the population. People start buying goods in more quantities than they do in anticipation of rising prices. This causes more people to start buying even more things for fear of missing out on essential goods and services. This causes prices to get out of control sometimes and hyperinflation occurs.

Options for Hyperinflation

If you ever find yourself in a country that is either experiencing hyperinflation, or it might soon, there are various steps you can take to protect yourself. As hyperinflation significantly erodes the value of the currency, commodities become expensive. The most in-demand items such as food, water, fuel, and utilities usually experience the highest increase in prices. Owning assets that produce these commodities, or owning these commodities outright is an excellent way to insulate yourself from the harmful effects of hyperinflation.

A lot of the strategies listed below are from the people who experienced hyperinflation in the Weimar Republic post World War I. This was the last case of hyperinflation in a developed country.

Owning Farmland or a Home Garden

There are several assets investors choose to turn to whenever investing in balancing out the effects of inflation. Gold is a popular and effective asset to consider. However, investing in a commodity such as owning farmland or home garden can pay off better than other asset classes.

In other words, the rising prices in food and other organics play a significant role in inflation. To benefit from this, investors invest in farmlands that pay off better during inflation. Higher prices would increase the value for crops, allowing the farmer to make up for higher rent expenses for the land.

Investors are more inclined than ever in owning home gardens or farmlands as the demand for food continues to rise while farmland supply decreases significantly. Investing in farmland is profitable as it offers constant returns as per historical evidence and effectively poses as a hedge against inflation measures.

Farmland is referred to as gold that can yield. Such an investment enables investors to be more exposed to opportunities for financial gain. The valuable commodities that are produced from the farmland give an edge over investing in other options available.

Converting Everything to Foreign Currency or Precious Metals

During hyperinflation, the average value of a country's currency decreases notably. Converting existing cash or owning foreign currency(ies) or precious metals is the smart option to opt for during hyperinflation. Owning top-performing assets can act as a hedge against hyperinflation and its severe consequences. In some cases, it might even be very profitable. Investors have been using the tactic of investing in precious metals to prevent themselves from adverse risks and financial repercussions.

The prices of precious metals rise higher during inflation and are relatively safe compared to other asset classes. Investors who sense incoming hyperinflation are quick to respond by investing in metals like gold and silver.

As the currency value decreases, the value of precious metals increases, depicting a negative correlation. These metals balance out the effects of inflation giving investors an upper hand even during times of a financial crisis.

Similarly, local currency can quickly lose its value, and investors often turn to store their money value by converting cash or liquid assets to foreign currencies. Converting everything into foreign currency can protect investors from the impacts of the devalued currency i.e., losing their current monetary value. The foreign exchange rates may vary based on the different inflation rates amongst the many currencies available.

Postponing Payment of Debt

With hyperinflation, you can expect to witness a decline in the average value of a country's currency that is undergoing a financial crisis. Money now is more valuable than what it will be in the future.

The value of debt decreases during hyperinflation; however, it can become quite challenging to pay off debts during hyperinflation. This is because inflation often has little to no effect on income. With a diminishing value of income, individuals will be spending more on sky-high goods and will have lesser disposable income to pay off debts. But delaying these payments will be a lot more beneficial since the debt will be worth less and less as the value of the local currency continues to decline.

A financial crisis would encourage businesses to delay payments by purchasing supplies on credit. These businesses prefer to delay their payment dates to incur a 'less valuable debt' during hyperinflation. Failure to obtain credit for a business during hyperinflation may be as severe as putting the firm out of business. You can also do the same and seek to delay payment of as much debt as is possible. This is because it will be a lot easier to pay off the debt in the future as the value of the currency in which the debt was taken would be significantly reduced. If you also invest in commodities or other assets to protect yourself against hyperinflation, you would be able to pay off the debt with much more ease in the future.

Getting into Long Term Financing

When an economy experiences hyperinflation, central banks usually raise interest rates to control inflation by reducing the money supply. This makes borrowing expensive in the short term. However, the important thing to note is that since all these loans will need to be paid back in the local currency, the loans will be worth much less in the future and consequently, much easier to pay off. This is because the currency would have significantly lost its value making it a lot easier to acquire from the sale of goods or property. For example, if you take out a mortgage from a bank in a period of an extremely high level of inflation, your monthly payments will be in the local currency. However, the value of your property will most likely appreciate monthly and will be worth many times more at the time of the mortgage's maturity. This is because you will be making the payments in the now heavily discounted local currency. A mortgage is one example. You can also take other forms of long-term financing. The basic idea is to buy commodities or assets that have the greatest potential of appreciating in value over time as the value of the currency in which the loan has been borrowed continues to decline.

The Risk of Government Intervention

During a traumatic experience like hyperinflation, there is tremendous pressure on the Government to mitigate the pain due to hyperinflation. This element is very unpredictable. For example, long term financing of apartments might make you think that it's a great think to be a landlord during hyperinflation. However, during the Weimar Republic hyperinflation, rents were capped by the Government, leading to many landlords going bust. During hyperinflation in Venezuela, it's natural for wheat and soy prices to rise. However, the Government imposed price controls which led to food shortages.

In Argentina, the Government outlawed exchange of Argentinian pesos for foreign currency.

The anonymous and decentralized nature of Bitcoin has proven to be a boon for those who held Bitcoin in Venezuela. Venezuelans have widely adopted use of Bitcoin in their daily life through P2P (Peer-to-Peer) networks. Other countries with high inflation problems (like Zimbabwe) have struggled to do so.

The unknown elements of hyperinflation make diversification especially important. You never know what is an asset during hyperinflation, and what is not.

Conclusion

Sectors that Outperform during Inflationary Periods

We have talked at length about the types of sectors that have traditionally performed very well during inflationary periods. These sectors can be traced back to the fundamentals upon which inflation is based. These fundamentals dictate that sectors that deal with goods that are in demand all year round are very likely to perform well during times of inflation. The reason being their ability to transfer the increase in the cost of their raw materials directly onto consumers because people always need what they are selling. These sectors commonly include food and beverage producers, agriculture companies, and healthcare providers.

Other sectors that perform really well during inflationary periods are those sectors that either produce or provide services to utility companies and energy providers. Examples include power generation companies and oil and gas companies, These sectors experience healthy appreciation in their stock prices during times of high inflation because they are directly related to the core energy requirements of the population.

The Importance of Diversification in a Portfolio

While we have discussed numerous ways through which you can confidently protect your finances against inflation, we would suggest not putting all of your eggs in one basket. The main reason for this is that even though all of the avenues we have discussed are quite effective at countering the effects of inflation if they are used together, their effects can become more certain.

There are countless combinations you can try to create a diverse portfolio to protect your investments. This is my favorite allocation.

10%	Precious metals
15%	Commodities
20%	High Quality Tech Investments
20%	Foreign stocks (non-US developed and emerging)
10%	Real estate (REIT's, REIM's)
10%	Speculation (Crypto / Mining Stocks)
15%	Cash in Multiple Currencies/Inflation Indexed Bonds

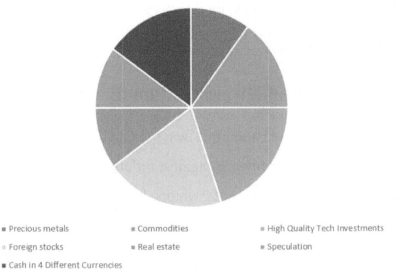

There are a few reasons why this specific combination is ideal.

- Firstly, because having stakes in commodities, tech investments, and foreign stocks ensure that more than 70% of your portfolio is highly liquid. This means that you can convert your holdings into and out of cash quickly and easily.

- Secondly, investing in precious metals, commodities, and real estate is almost guaranteed to perform well during inflationary periods even if the other assets in your portfolio do not or take a while to catch up with the others in terms of value appreciation.

- Thirdly, because investing 10% in speculative instruments provides a little risk exposure to your portfolio which can produce more than average results but even if it underperforms, it will still be only 10% or less which means that more than 90

  % of your portfolio will be relatively safer and will go on to ensure that the entire portfolio makes a decent return.

- And lastly, a 10% investment in real estate provides much-needed strength to the portfolio as real estate almost always performs well in the long term. Because this is not as liquid as the others, you will be less likely to trade it more frequently which will ensure that your portfolio has a long-term appreciating asset as well.

Other Resources

As you come to the end of this book, I hope you realize that we only wish the best of success in your investing journey. Whether you utilize my strategies or not, we want you to do well.

Here are a few other resources that I recommend for investors:

Rule #1 Investing – This is hands down the best investing book I have ever read. Helps value investors which stocks are priced below their true value and buy a stock at a good Margin of Safety.

Investing QuickStart Guide – Great resource for beginner investors to get started with investing.

The Dando Investor – Another great investing resource

The Downfall of Money – A fantastic, detailed story of the finances during the Weimar Republic's hyperinflation in the 1920s

The end... almost!

Reviews are not easy to come by.

As an independent author with a tiny marketing budget, I rely on readers, like you, to leave a short review on Amazon.

Even if it's just a sentence or two!

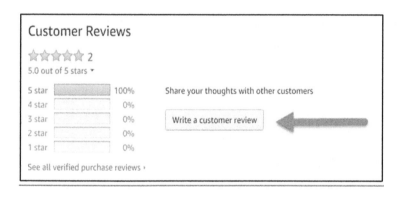

So if you enjoyed the book, please...

I am very appreciative for your review as it truly makes a difference.

Thank you from the bottom of my heart for purchasing this book and reading it to the end.